OBAMA - GUILTY

OF BEING PRESIDENT WHILE BLACK

Other works by D T Pollard

**Rooftop Diva – A Novel of Triumph
After Katrina (fiction)**

**Fools' Heaven – Love, Lust and
Death Beyond the Pulpit (fiction)**

**TARP TOWN U S A – The
Recession That Saved America**

OBAMA - GUILTY
OF BEING PRESIDENT WHILE BLACK

D T Pollard

Book Express

Book Express books may be ordered through
booksellers or by contacting

Book Express
P.O. Box 541651
Grand Prairie, TX 75052
www.DTPollard.com
dtpollard@dtpollard.com

This is a work of non-fiction
isbn: 978-0-9824606-2-7 (pbk)
isbn: 978-0-9824606-3-4 (ebk)

.

First Printing

Printed in the United States of America

This book is dedicated to everyone who was alive to witness the United States of America elect its first African American President.

This book is also dedicated to everyone who gave their lives for the cause of freedom and never imagined that the United States of America would ever elect an African American as President.

INTRODUCTION

♦

OBAMA – GUILTY of Being President While Black is an inspiration that came to me after witnessing the disrespect and venom expressed towards President Obama during the health-care debates.

Barack Obama received a mandate in the general election. Several months later, it was a strange sight to witness people gathered around town-hall meeting sites bearing signs depicting the President as Hitler, a socialist or a tyrant. Some even carried guns. Something much deeper was at play with President Obama and it centered on his race.

Those who did not vote for Obama during the presidential election had many reasons for supporting Senator John McCain. Some of the votes that went against the victor in the general election were because of an inability of many to vote for a black man.

Exit polling data indicated an increase in the proportion of white voters who supported John McCain versus the percentage that voted for John Kerry in 2004. Obama's loss of most southern states and many sparsely populated states in the middle of the country displayed a racial schism in voting patterns. In states all across the nation the election map bore out similar patterns with blue counties in and around urban areas that supported Obama surrounded by a sea of red counties that went for McCain. That split later expressed itself with angry outbursts by individual citizens and some members of the media.

D T Pollard

Chapter 1

♦

How did the United States of America end up with an illegal-alien Kenyan socialist who palled around with a terrorist and wanted to euthanize your grandmother to save money as President? Hold on a minute. None of that was true! Oh, now I understand. Barack Obama was simply found guilty of Being President While Black.

One thing that I know like the back of my hand is what it is like to be a black man in America. I have been in that position all of my life due to the circumstances of my birth. I also had the added experience of growing up in a small town in the south and living my entire life in the southern United States. Given that backdrop, imagine how I felt when Barack Hussein Obama became the forty-fourth President of the United States on November 5, 2008.

My initial emotions were pride, elation and disbelief that the United States finally crossed a line I thought I would not live to see. My second thoughts were, "Now we will bear witness to what it is like to be Guilty of Being President While Black."

That reality was a story yet to fully unfold, but the early experience portended a dark future. People gathered outside presidential meetings with guns, yelling defamatory slogans, engaging in mockery and openly verbalizing expressions of wishes for the failure of President Obama. The prior actions all occurred within eight months of his inauguration. What does the future hold? A dark concentrated cloud of hate hung low. On Monday, August 31, 2009, the following was posted on the website foxnews.com:

A Phoenix-area pastor has started to draw protesters to his congregation after he delivered a sermon titled, "Why I Hate Barack Obama," and told his parishioners that he prays for President Obama's death.

Pastor Steven Anderson stood by his sermon in an interview with MyFOXPhoenix, which reports that the pastor continues to encourage his parishioners to join him in praying for the president's death.

"I hope that God strikes Barack Obama with brain cancer so he can die like Ted Kennedy and I hope it happens today," he told MyFOXPhoenix on Sunday. He called his message "spiritual warfare" and said he does not condone killing.

In his sermon, Anderson stated:

"I'm gonna pray that he dies and goes to hell when I go to bed tonight. That's what I'm gonna pray," he told his congregation.

Did we really know to expect such raw reactions from Obama's harshest critics? We had some idea because Barack Obama had previously been placed on trial for Running For President While Black. You remember that process. It was like a prolonged training camp in the event he actually won the election. Let us recap some of the highlights of Obama's presidential boot camp.

How could we forget the dropped jaws when Obama won the Iowa primary caucuses? The reality that a state that could have placed its black residents on the back of milk cartons actually voted for a black man shocked the country. Endless analysis and a realization that this guy might be a threat to win started to creep into people's minds.

The pressure was immediately ratcheted up on Barack Obama to see if he could withstand the heat. The supposed death blow was the tossing of the Reverend Wright radical-black-preacher bomb into the living rooms of America. Endless looping of a few seconds of out of context sound bites and subsequent wall-to-wall coverage of two live speeches of Reverend Jeremiah Wright should have done the trick. Not so, Obama deftly turned the bombastic Reverend episode into a national speech about race in America. He later cut ties with his former pastor and moved on.

It had to happen. The obvious reminder that Barack Obama was a black candidate came in South Carolina. Former President Bill Clinton reminded everyone that Reverend Jesse Jackson also won that state's primary when he ran for President. The implication of Clinton's statement was that the large black Democratic Party voting pool had more to do with Obama's victory than his appeal as a general election candidate. Bill Clinton was still smarting from the endorsement that the late Senator Edward Kennedy gave to Barack Obama instead of Hillary Clinton.

Obama was also portrayed as being less ready to be commander-in-chief than the leading Republican rival, Senator John McCain. A so-called commander-in-chief threshold was mentioned. It was never clear what the threshold was or how to cross it.

Obama defied all logic and rewrote the rules of presidential politics. His message of change and hope struck a chord with the American people. Tens of thousands flocked to his rallies in every city he campaigned in. The audiences he drew looked like America as it was meant to be and included members from every age, race, gender and religious group in the country. That diverse coalition lifted Barack Obama from the Senate and placed him into the White House. How did that broad support give way to the contempt that was openly expressed mere months later?

Near the end of the Democratic Primary contest, after Obama had all but locked up the nomination, the racial divide exposed itself as states such as West Virginia and Kentucky soundly rejected the frontrunner in favor of his rival, Senator Hillary Clinton. After a protracted campaign that spanned almost two years, Barack Obama became the first black person to win the nomination for President of a major American political party. Little did he know, the fun was only about to begin.

One of the Democratic Party's new standard bearer's first rewards was being featured on the cover of the New Yorker magazine. The cover was a cartoon depicting Barack Obama wearing a turban and Middle Eastern garb while he bumped fists with his wife who had a gun hung on her back. In the background an American flag was burning in a fireplace. The magazine termed it satire while many others said it was outrageous.

As a back story, the fist bump referred to a gesture that Barack Obama performed with his wife Michelle on stage when it was obvious that his Democratic primary pledged-delegate lead could not be overcome. Obama bumped fists with his wife as a gesture of affirmation. A commentator for Fox News termed the gesture a terrorist fist jab. Even innocent interactions were painted as somehow nefarious.

Chapter 2

♦

The Democratic National Convention was held in Denver, Colorado August 25 through August 28, 2008, and was a huge success. The convention culminated with Barack Obama emerging onto the stage framed by a backdrop of faux Greek columns as he spoke to accept the formal nomination for President.

It seemed that the die was cast. How could a lackluster Republican opponent, Senator John McCain, manage to compete with the compelling presence of Barack Obama? The country did not have long to wait as the Republican National Convention started the next week in St. Paul, Minnesota.

John McCain had yet to announce his running mate and it seemed that a pair of less than exciting personalities would be paired to run against the Obama-Biden juggernaut.

The Republican National Convention appeared to be doomed from the onset. There seemed to be an all-out effort to avoid bringing the largely unpopular Republican President, George W. Bush, to St. Paul and Mother Nature gave an assist by sending Hurricane Gustav perilously close to Katrina-ravaged New Orleans, Louisiana. Gustav gave the Republicans cover to cancel part of the schedule which took care of any possible live appearances by President George W. Bush and Vice-President Richard Cheney.

The bombshell that would transform the Republican convention from a snooze fest into the only show worth watching was yet to come and it was not John McCain. Seemingly out of nowhere John McCain announced that his choice for a running mate was obscure Alaska Governor Sarah Palin.

The frenzied media was sent into overdrive as they rushed to find out exactly what this relatively young and inexperienced Governor was all about. Sarah Palin walked onto the stage at the Republican National Convention and made as good of a first impression as someone unknown could on fervent Republican supporters.

Palin was rolled out as a package with her husband and five children in tow. Her background and physical presence of being a former beauty queen presented a set of contradictions not encountered before on the national political stage.

Sarah Palin was not just a mere whim of a selection, but was designed to be a potential landmine for Barack Obama to step on if he was not disciplined enough. She also was a shiny lure for the disaffected supporters of Hillary Clinton. Most of all, Sarah Palin was the equivalent of a human shield for the Republican Party. She was sent out to hurl stones at Barack Obama and almost dared him to fight back with full knowledge of the consequences. Obama had survived one campaign against Hillary Clinton that was laced with all manner of racial, social and historical black man to white woman traps that he managed to avoid.

With a short two-month window before election-day it was questionable if enough could be discovered about this unknown governor from Alaska to demystify the image that was thrust upon the voting public of this strong, compelling and focused symbol for women.

Two months could be a long time, particularly if it was spent under a microscope as the media was trying to unravel the mystery of a newcomer to the national political scene. Sarah Palin could be a heartbeat away from the presidency with a President possessing a history of skin cancer if John McCain won the election.

The first chink in her armor was an interview with Charles Gibson of ABC News when she could not come up with a definition or opinion on the Bush Doctrine when asked. Another interview with Katie Couric of CBS News proved to be a disaster when Palin was unable to come up with the names of newspapers that she read to stay informed on current issues of the day among other lapses. After the Couric interview many voters discounted her preparedness to be a heartbeat away from the presidency of the United States.

Palin threw fire bombs at Barack Obama while John McCain stayed largely above the fray. It was Palin who painted Obama as someone who palled around with a domestic terrorist. It was Palin who threw around the word socialist when referring to Barack Obama. Palin worked the rural areas that loved her act. She was a rock star for the "Real-Americans" as defined by the Republican Party of 2008.

Obama steered clear of the numerous pitfalls by largely ignoring the Alaska governor and allowed her to implode under the weight of her professional and personal issues. I feel there was one lasting legacy of Sarah Palin's national campaign. Sarah Palin created a poisoned pool in those areas that were unlikely to vote for Barack Obama under any circumstances. We would harvest the bitter fruit of that resentment from those people later.

Then unexpectedly a story appeared in the Pittsburg-Tribune Review by Jill King Greenwood on Thursday, October 23, 2008, which was less than two weeks away from the election. The story stated:

A knife-wielding man robbed a McCain-Palin campaign volunteer and etched a "B" into her face after he saw a McCain bumper sticker on the woman's car, Pittsburgh police said.

Ashley Todd, 20, of College Station, Texas, was using an ATM at Liberty Avenue and Pearl Street in Bloomfield just before 9 p.m. Wednesday when a man approached her, put a knife to her throat and demanded $60, police said.

Todd handed the man $60 she had in her pocket and stepped away from him, investigators said. The man then noticed the bumper sticker on the woman's car, which was parked in front of the ATM. The man became very angry, made comments to Todd about John McCain and punched her in the back of the head, knocking her to the ground, police said.

"He continued to kick and punch her repeatedly and said he would teach her a lesson for supporting John McCain," said police Chief Nate Harper.

The man then carved the "B" into Todd's right cheek. Todd, who isn't familiar with the area, drove to a friend's house nearby and told her friend she wasn't sure of the exact location where the robbery took place but remembered a green sign above the ATM. The friend called police and the officer met them on Cypress Street in Bloomfield, police said.

Later in the article, the alleged victim gave a description of her assailant which is printed below:

Police described the suspect as black, about 6-foot-4, and said he was wearing dark-colored jeans and a black undershirt.

That sensational story burned through the media like a wildfire, but there was something wrong that raised doubts immediately. The B that was carved on the young woman's face was reversed as if done while looking at a reflection in a mirror. Todd's story quickly fell apart. She admitted that she made the story up but could not remember if she scratched the letter on her face or if someone else did it. While that young woman seemed to have issues that needed to be addressed, some didn't hesitate to try and turn that incident into a political advantage. A McCain campaign aide in Pennsylvania related to the press that the B carved onto the woman's face stood for "Barack" according to sources familiar with the story.

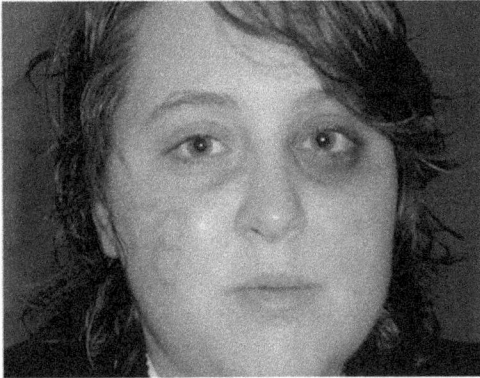

Photo of woman who was a
Republican volunteer and fabricated a
story of   being attacked by a large
black man who robbed her and
became enraged when he noticed a
McCain bumper sticker on   her car.
She claimed that the man then carved
a B on her face.

This was the ultimate attempt to affix guilt by association. Within two weeks of the presidential election, the skeleton of "a big-black man attacks helpless white woman" was drug out of the closet and tossed into the middle of the political room. Even if the story was a hoax, its intent was clear. That incident was an attempt to drop a racial carpet bomb that would engulf Barack Obama in a nationwide racial backlash from enraged and frightened white voters. It did not work that time.

That was not the first time race had been injected into a political campaign in an attempt to poison the voting pool. Democratic Candidate Michael Dukakis was hit with an advertisement featuring convicted felon Willie Horton, a black man, who went on a crime spree while participating in a weekend furlough program. Dukakis had supported the program when he was the Governor of Massachusetts. Ironically, John McCain was the subject of a racially motivated smear campaign when he ran against George W. Bush in the Republican primaries in 2000. McCain was accused of fathering a black child out of wedlock, when in fact the girl was his adopted daughter from Bangladesh.

An unknown number of black men paid with their lives over the years after real, imagined and fabricated incidents involving interactions with white women throughout the history of this country. One well known example was Emmitt Till, who was 14 when he was murdered in Money, Mississippi in 1955 for reportedly whistling at a white woman. We had finally reached a point where righteous skepticism overruled kneejerk reaction and this fraud was exposed for what it was. In the end, it was just another strange racially-charged incident that emerged during the historic presidential race of 2008.

Chapter 3

♦

As I have mentioned before I have a great deal of experience being a black man in America. There have been retail store clerks not wanting to touch my hands when giving change. I have been followed while shopping in retail stores and ignored as someone else was waited on even if I came in first. The true rite of passage is being stopped for D W B also known as driving while black. I have experienced two particularly vivid incidents of that in my past.

One occurrence was the post-visual identification stop. That is when you are pulled over only after the officer clearly identifies that this is someone he should stop based upon the driver and automobile combination. The second was a supposed call-in of a vehicle driving too slow at night. After finding no valid reason for the stop, the police officer apologized and moved on.

Now in the case of President Obama, he was being asked to produce an original long-form birth certificate. His critics had literally pulled the White House over and demanded to see the President's papers. That questioned the very basis of his legal standing to be President of the United States. Now this "Birther" group, as they were being labeled, included elected members of Congress and a few mainstream cable news personalities. Obama's opponent during the general election, Senator John McCain, was actually born in a foreign country. John McCain was born in the Panama Canal Zone. An article By Carl Hulse Published: February 28, 2008, in The New York Times states: "Mr. McCain was born on a military installation in the Canal Zone, where his mother and father, a Navy officer, were stationed. McCain's legitimacy to be President was never seriously questioned."

The United States Constitution reads as follows regarding the Presidency:

No person except a natural born Citizen, or a Citizen of the United States, at the time of the Adoption of this Constitution, shall be eligible to the Office of President; neither shall any

Person be eligible to that Office who shall not have attained to the Age of thirty-five Years, and been fourteen Years a Resident within the United States.

The Constitution is a document that is over 200-years old and frozen in time in many respects. There have been many amendments over the years, but the term natural-born citizen does not have a finite definition. It is only speculation to try and determine the real intent of the term natural-born citizen. It was clear John McCain was more questionable as a legitimate contender for President than Obama concerning his country of birth. Of course the birth certificate nonsense was meant to define President Obama as the ultimate other. The lengths that the Birther contingent would go to became evident on August 3, 2009, when an obviously forged Barack Obama Kenyan birth certificate began circulating around the internet. According to The Huffington Post, some of the document's flaws were as follows:

Kenya was a Dominion the date this certificate was allegedly issued and would not become a republic for 8 months.

Mombasa belonged to Zanzibar when Obama was born, not Kenya.

Obama's father's village would be nearer to Nairobi, not Mombasa.

The number 47O44-- 47 is Obama's age when he became president, followed by the letter O (not a zero) followed by 44--he is the 44th president.

The fake birth certificate listed Kenya as a republic before it was a republic.

On the following page is an image of the faked Kenyan Obama birth certificate that "Birthers" seized upon as genuine. It turned out to be a hoax from Australia. The Birthers thought they had found a way to constitutionally disqualify Barack Obama from being President and overturn the 2008 election results.

7s. 6d.   № 495   COAST ⬥ PROVINCE

CERTIFIED COPY OF REGISTRATION OF BIRTH

19 __   No. _____   DISTRICT OF _____   ____

Date and Place of Birth	4th August, 1961 at Coast General Hospital, Mombasa
Christian Names	BARACK HUSSEIN II ___ Male
FATHER— Name, Surname, Age, and Birthplace	Barack Hussein OBAMA 26 years Kanyadhiang village, Kenya Province
Occupation	Student
MOTHER— Name, Surname, Maiden Surname, Age, and Birthplace	Stanley Ann OBAMA formerly DUNHAM 18 years Wichita, Kansas, UNITED STATES
Year of Present Marriage	1961
Number of Previous Issue { Living { Deceased	nil nil
Signature, Description and Residence of Informant	B.H. OBAMA, Father Student, Hawaii, UNITED STATES
Signature of Registrar	E.T. Lavender
Date of Registration	4th August, 1961
(For official use only)	

Entered at the District Registry Office, this 4th day of August, 1961

E. Miller
District Registrar

I, _____ Joshua Simon COUMA _____, Deputy Registrar of Births, Deaths, and Marriages for the Coast Province of Kenya, do hereby certify that the above is a true copy of the entry recorded in the Birth Register of this Province, Book ___, Page ___.

Given under my Hand and Seal of Office this 17th day of February, 1964

Deputy Registrar

OFFICE OF THE PRINCIPAL REGISTRAR,
COAST PROVINCE, REPUBLIC OF KENYA

This was a dangerous time to be an "other" with the economy in meltdown mode. The economy went over a cliff in October of 2008, and was hanging on by a bumper caught on a rock when Barack Obama was poised to assume the highest public office in the land on Tuesday January 20, 2009. On Friday January 16, conservative radio talk-show host Rush Limbaugh proclaimed to his millions of listeners that he hoped that Obama would fail. That was the backdrop for the upcoming presidential inauguration.

Bush passed the keys over to Obama on January 20, 2009. Whenever there is a business downturn and people are losing jobs, the easiest thing to do is blame "the others" that are taking your piece of the pie. That was not new and comes around like clockwork when times get tough. After seven months in office, Obama was faulted for not having repaired eight-years of damage perpetrated by the previous administration. The bulging bank accounts of Wall Street and bank executives, reflective of the greed that stripped the middle class clean, did not all occur since January 2009.

With the economy ready to plunge into the abyss, it was going to require a tremendous effort to pull the country from the brink.

Let us examine the circular logic of blaming the guy who was forced to clean up what the last administration broke.

"Hey Obama, have you fixed the economy yet?"

I understood the lack of patience from a public that had lost millions of jobs as consumer demand took a nosedive. I empathize with laid-off workers on the verge of having their unemployment benefits end. I urge those in states with governors who rejected federal stimulus money designated to extend unemployment assistance to hold them accountable. Their choice to reject help from the stimulus package was based upon political grandstanding instead of genuine concern for the citizens who elected them to govern wisely.

The Republican Party continued to just say no without any real ideas of their own to bring to the table. As the domestic automobile industry teetered on the edge of collapse, President Obama pressed forward with plans to help the industry survive. Many Republicans praised the virtues of foreign automobile assembly plants located in their states and seemed willing to allow American based automobile manufacturing to fail. Much of that opposition was not logical and the race of the President could have been a major factor of why they opposed everything he proposed. When Obama reached his hand across the aisle it was promptly slapped away.

Next, I want to go into a few things aimed at the President of the United States that seemed to come right out of our shameful

Jim Crow past. Within seven months, Barack Obama went from a landslide election victory and became the most disrespected President in modern history.

Chapter 4

♦

Barack Obama assumed the office of President on January 20, 2009, and it did not take long before shocking racial insults were hurled at the leader of the free world.

Barack Obama was not a stranger to racist characterizations while he was competing for the Democratic nomination. During June of 2008, a company out of Utah created an Obama Sock Monkey that was sold via the internet. A subsequent uproar caused the product to be pulled off the market quickly. However a recent check that I performed in August of 2009, directed me to a website selling both an Obama and Biden sock monkey and it appeared to be functional.

Obama Sock Monkey

One particular label that would be attached to candidate Obama and subsequent to President Obama was that of "Magic Negro." The first time I can document the Magic Negro tag for Barack Obama was in a Los Angeles Times article on March 19, 2007. According to the article the "Magic Negro" is essentially a less threatening black figure who is there to assuage minimal white guilt about the country's history of slavery and racial segregation.

"He has no past, he simply appears one day to help the white protagonist," reads the description on Wikipedia.org.

While this is obviously a demeaning racial slur, it took on a life of its own and spawned a musical variation. The song "Barack The Magic Negro" was created by conservative satirist Paul Shanklin and set to the tune of the children's song "Puff The Magic Dragon." During March of 2007, conservative radio host Rush Limbaugh played Shanklin's song, Barack The Magic Negro" nationwide over the public airwaves on his radio broadcast. Did Limbaugh suffer the fate of Don Imus who was taken off the air after he made comments about the Rutgers Women's basketball team? The answer is no. The reason nothing happened to Limbaugh is that anyone who was outraged did not matter because they were not a part of his listening audience. In fact, Limbaugh was probably seen as feeding red meat to his loyal fan base.

The "Barack The Magic Negro" episode did not end there and crept into the political mainstream. Chip Saltsman, a candidate running for the chairmanship of the Republican National Committee, sent out compact discs to committee members containing the song Barack The Magic Negro as Christmas gifts during December of 2008. The idea that someone running to lead the national organization of the opposition party to the President-elect of the United States would so disrespect the incoming President was mind boggling. What was even more shocking was how he found nothing wrong with the tone of the song to begin with.

Then there was the infamous New York Post cartoon with two policemen looking at a dead chimp while one of them held a smoking gun. It ignited a firestorm of criticism. The caption stated, "They'll have to find someone else to write the next stimulus bill." The interpretation of the cartoon was left up to the viewer and many saw it as a racist jab at Barack Obama.

Another unbelievable act of racial disrespect occurred in February 2009. A mayor of a town in California circulated an email with a graphic showing the White House lawn planted with watermelons. A caption under the image stated "No Easter egg hunt this year." On August 4, 2009, an image of President Obama with the makeup of the Joker from the movie The Dark Knight appeared all around Los Angeles, California. I am reminded of the time I was driving from Texas to Florida and stopped at a service station in Alabama in the late 1980s. When I pulled up to park a group of ceramic mammy figurines wearing red headscarves greeted me from behind a display window.

Just why was the anger and disrespect so deep for our first African American President? The answer rested in our dark past of racial segregation and that is what we will revisit next in order to understand the backlash of the present.

White House watermelon patch image

Emailed by
former mayor
of Los Alamitos, Ca. Dean Grose
February 24, 2009

Chapter 5

_____

♦

In order to understand why some in this country were so incensed that Barack Obama was President you need to understand the position of African Americans in this country less than two generations ago. I want everyone and especially young people to know that there was a time that black citizens were seen as a group with far less than equal legal standing when compared to white Americans.

The following information is from **the Martin Luther King, Jr. National Historic Site (National Park Service)** and gives a great overview of something called Jim Crow. Once you understand how black people were regulated in certain regions of this nation, you will understand where the disrespect of Barack Obama emanates. The United States now has a President that many in this country view as less of a person than they are.

From the 1880s into the 1960s, a majority of American states enforced segregation through "Jim Crow" laws (so called after a black character in minstrel shows). From Delaware to California, and from North Dakota to Texas, many states (and cities, too) could impose legal punishments on people for consorting with members of another race. The most common types of laws forbade intermarriage and ordered business owners and public institutions to keep their black and white clientele separated. Here is a sampling of laws from various states.

Nurses: No person or corporation shall require any white female nurse to nurse in wards or rooms in hospitals, either public or private, in which negro men are placed. *Alabama*

Buses: All passenger stations in this state operated by any motor transportation company shall have separate waiting rooms or space and separate ticket windows for the white and colored races. *Alabama*

Railroads: The conductor of each passenger train is authorized and required to assign each passenger to the car or the division of the car, when it is divided by a partition, designated for the race to which such passenger belongs. *Alabama*

Restaurants: It shall be unlawful to conduct a restaurant or other place for the serving of food in the city, at which white and colored people are served in the same room, unless such white and colored persons are effectually separated by a solid partition extending from the floor upward to a distance of seven feet or higher, and unless a separate entrance from the street is provided for each compartment. *Alabama*

Pool and Billiard Rooms: It shall be unlawful for a negro and white person to play together or in company with each other at any game of pool or billiards. *Alabama*

Toilet Facilities, Male: Every employer of white or negro males shall provide for such white or negro males reasonably accessible and separate toilet facilities. *Alabama*

Intermarriage: The marriage of a person of Caucasian blood with a Negro, Mongolian, Malay, or Hindu shall be null and void.   *Arizona*

Intermarriage: All marriages between a white person and a negro, or between a white person and a person of negro descent to the fourth generation inclusive, are hereby forever prohibited. *Florida*

Cohabitation: Any negro man and white woman, or any white man and negro woman, who are not married to each other, who shall habitually live in and occupy in the nighttime the same room shall each be punished by imprisonment not exceeding twelve (12) months, or by fine not exceeding five hundred ($500.00) dollars. *Florida*

Education: The schools for white children and the schools for negro children shall be conducted separately. *Florida*

Juvenile Delinquents: There shall be separate buildings, not nearer than one fourth mile to each other, one for white boys and one for negro boys. White boys and negro boys shall not, in any manner, be associated together or worked together. *Florida*

Mental Hospitals: The Board of Control shall see that proper and distinct apartments are arranged for said patients, so that in no case shall Negroes and white persons be together. *Georgia*

Intermarriage: It shall be unlawful for a white person to marry anyone except a white person. Any marriage in violation of this section shall be void. *Georgia*

Barbers: No colored barber shall serve as a barber [to] white women or girls. *Georgia*

Burial: The officer in charge shall not bury, or allow to be buried, any colored persons upon ground set apart or used for the burial of white persons. *Georgia*

Restaurants: All persons licensed to conduct a restaurant, shall serve either white people exclusively or colored people exclusively and shall not sell to the two races within the same room or serve the two races anywhere under the same license. *Georgia*

Amateur Baseball: It shall be unlawful for any amateur white baseball team to play baseball on any vacant lot or baseball diamond within two blocks of a playground devoted to the Negro race, and it shall be unlawful for any amateur colored baseball team to play baseball in any vacant lot or baseball diamond within two blocks of any playground devoted to the white race. *Georgia*

Parks: It shall be unlawful for colored people to frequent any park owned or maintained by the city for the benefit, use and enjoyment of white persons...and unlawful for any white person to frequent any park owned or maintained by the city for the use and benefit of colored persons. *Georgia*

Wine and Beer: All persons licensed to conduct the business of selling beer or wine...shall serve either white people exclusively or colored people exclusively and shall not sell to the two races within the same room at any time. *Georgia*

Reform Schools: The children of white and colored races committed to the houses of reform shall be kept entirely separate from each other. *Kentucky*

Circus Tickets: All circuses, shows, and tent exhibitions, to which the attendance of...more than one race is invited or expected to attend shall provide for the convenience of its patrons not less than two ticket offices with individual ticket sellers, and not less than two entrances to the said performance, with individual ticket takers and receivers, and in the case of outside or tent performances, the said ticket offices shall not be less than twenty-five (25) feet apart. *Louisiana*

Housing: Any person...who shall rent any part of any such building to a negro person or a negro family when such building is already in whole or in part in occupancy by a white person or white family, or vice versa when the building is in occupancy by a negro person or negro family, shall be guilty of a misdemeanor and on conviction thereof shall be punished by a fine of not less than twenty-five ($25.00) nor more than one hundred ($100.00) dollars or be imprisoned not less than 10, or more than 60 days, or both such fine and imprisonment in the discretion of the court. Louisiana

The Blind: The board of trustees shall...maintain a separate building...on separate ground for the admission, care, instruction, and support of all blind persons of the colored or black race. *Louisiana*

Intermarriage: All marriages between a white person and a negro, or between a white person and a person of negro descent, to the third generation, inclusive, or between a white person and a member of the Malay race; or between the negro and a member of the Malay race; or between a person of Negro descent, to the third generation, inclusive, and a member of the Malay race, are forever prohibited, and shall be void. *Maryland*

Railroads: All railroad companies and corporations, and all persons running or operating cars or coaches by steam on any railroad line or track in the State of Maryland, for the transportation of passengers, are hereby required to provide separate cars or coaches for the travel and transportation of the white and colored passengers. *Maryland*

Education: Separate schools shall be maintained for the children of the white and colored races. *Mississippi*

Promotion of Equality: Any person...who shall be guilty of printing, publishing or circulating printed, typewritten or written matter urging or presenting for public acceptance or general information, arguments or suggestions in favor of social equality or of intermarriage between whites and negroes, shall be guilty of a misdemeanor and subject to fine or not exceeding five hundred (500.00) dollars or imprisonment not exceeding six (6) months or both. *Mississippi*

Intermarriage: The marriage of a white person with a negro or mulatto or person who shall have one-eighth or more of negro blood, shall be unlawful and void. *Mississippi*

Hospital Entrances: There shall be maintained by the governing authorities of every hospital maintained by the state for treatment of white and colored patients separate entrances for white and colored patients and visitors, and such entrances shall be used by the race only for which they are prepared. *Mississippi*

Prisons: The warden shall see that the white convicts shall have separate apartments for both eating and sleeping from the negro convicts. Mississippi

Education: Separate free schools shall be established for the education of children of African descent; and it shall be unlawful for any colored child to attend any white school, or any white child to attend a colored school. *Missouri*

Intermarriage: All marriages between...white persons and negroes or white persons and Mongolians...are prohibited and declared absolutely void...No person having one-eighth part or more of negro blood shall be permitted to marry any white person, nor shall any white person be permitted to marry any negro or person having one-eighth part or more of negro blood. *Missouri*

Education: Separate rooms [shall] be provided for the teaching of pupils of African descent, and [when] said rooms are so provided, such pupils may not be admitted to the school rooms occupied and used by pupils of Caucasian or other descent. *New Mexico*

Textbooks: Books shall not be interchangeable between the white and colored schools, but shall continue to be used by the race first using them. *North Carolina*

Libraries: The state librarian is directed to fit up and maintain a separate place for the use of the colored people who may come to the library for the purpose of reading books or periodicals. *North Carolina*

Militia: The white and colored militia shall be separately enrolled, and shall never be compelled to serve in the same organization.No organization of colored troops shall be permitted where white troops are available, and while white permitted to be organized, colored troops shall be under the command of white officers. *North Carolina*

Transportation: The...Utilities Commission...is empowered and directed to require the establishment of separate waiting rooms at all stations for the white and colored races. *North Carolina*

Teaching: Any instructor who shall teach in any school, college or institution where members of the white and colored race are received and enrolled as pupils for

instruction shall be deemed guilty of a
misdemeanor, and upon conviction thereof,
shall be fined in any sum not less than ten
dollars ($10.00) nor more than fifty dollars
($50.00) for each offense. *Oklahoma*

Fishing, Boating, and Bathing: The
[Conservation] Commission shall have the
right to make segregation of the white and
colored races as to the exercise of rights of
fishing, boating and bathing. *Oklahoma*

Mining: The baths and lockers for the
negroes shall be separate from the white race,
but may be in the same building. *Oklahoma*

Telephone Booths: The Corporation
Commission is hereby vested with power and
authority to require telephone companies...to
maintain separate booths for white and
colored patrons when there is a demand for
such separate booths. That the Corporation
Commission shall determine the necessity for
said separate booths only upon complaint of
the people in the town and vicinity to be
served after due hearing as now provided by
law in other complaints filed with the
Corporation Commission. *Oklahoma*

Lunch Counters: No persons, firms,
or corporations, who or which furnish meals
to passengers at station restaurants or station
eating houses, in times limited by common

carriers of said passengers, shall furnish said meals to white and colored passengers in the same room, or at the same table, or at the same counter. *South Carolina*

Child Custody: It shall be unlawful for any parent, relative, or other white person in this State, having the control or custody of any white child, by right of guardianship, natural or acquired, or otherwise, to dispose of, give or surrender such white child permanently into the custody, control, maintenance, or support, of a negro. *South Carolina*

Libraries: Any white person of such county may use the county free library under the rules and regulations prescribed by the commissioners court and may be entitled to all the privileges thereof. Said court shall make proper provision for the negroes of said county to be served through a separate branch or branches of the county free library, which shall be administered by [a] custodian of the negro race under the supervision of the county librarian. *Texas*

Education: [The County Board of Education] shall provide schools of two kinds; those for white children and those for colored children. *Texas*

Theaters: Every person...operating...any public hall, theatre, opera house, motion picture show or any place of public entertainment or public assemblage which is attended by both white and colored persons, shall separate the white race and the colored race and shall set apart and designate...certain seats therein to be occupied by white persons and a portion thereof , or certain seats therein, to be occupied by colored persons. *Virginia*

Railroads: The   conductors   or managers on all such railroads shall have power, and are hereby required, to assign to each white or colored passenger his or her respective car, coach or compartment. If the passenger fails to disclose his race, the conductor and managers, acting in good faith, shall be the sole judges of his race. *Virginia*

Intermarriage: All marriages of white persons with Negroes, Mulattos, Mongolians, or Malaya hereafter contracted in the State of Wyoming are and shall be illegal and void. *Wyoming*

The prior information regarding the oppressive Jim Crow laws demonstrate how they regulated the interaction between blacks and whites. The list of laws also illustrates how those laws clearly were not a strictly southern states issue, but they generally were enforced more aggressively in southern states. It should also help explain why there is a disproportionate amount of anger and distrust of President Obama in the southern United States. I believe that this attitude towards the President is a result of residual remnants of Jim Crow. If a group of people were legally deemed less equal for a long period of time, it could be a difficult idea to relinquish.

The long shadow of racial segregation could be why, according to Ronald Kessler, author of In the President's Secret Service, President Barack Obama receives 30 death threats daily.

President Obama as the Joker

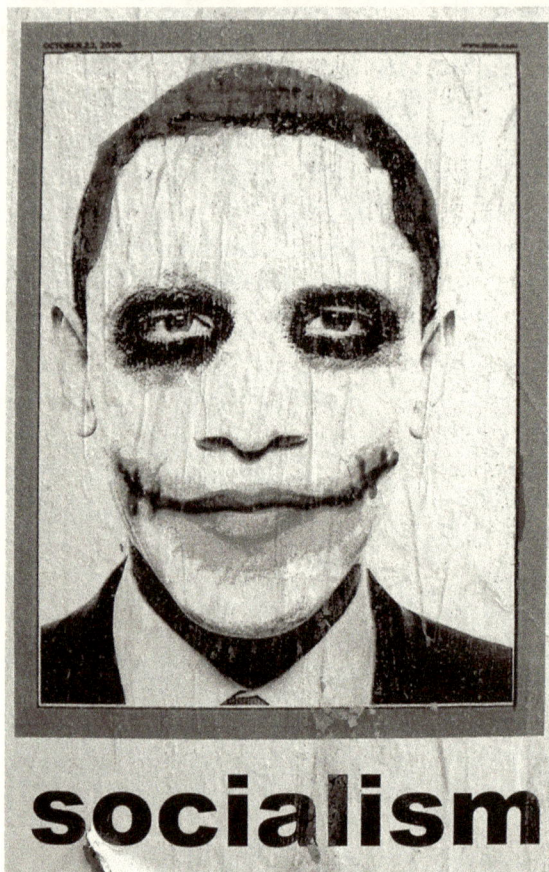

Posters appeared in Los Angeles

Chapter 6

♦

Barack Obama was almost custom tailored for his critics to be able to exploit almost every fear and phobia his opponents might possess. Most prominent is the fact that he is the offspring of a union between a black man and a white woman. That was the holy grail of transgressions under Jim Crow. Secondly he lived for a period of time in Indonesia which amounted to a permission slip to push the secret-radical-extremist button. The third convenient fact is his father was a Kenyan and that gave rise to the not quite American plotline.

One illustration was a Research 2000 Poll commissioned by Daily Kos and published July 31, 2009, on the Dailykos.com website.

The question was, **Do you believe that Barack Obama was born in the United States of America or not?** The answers were stunning. Those that said yes were broken down along regional and party lines. Overall 77 percent said yes, 11 percent said no and 12 percent were not sure. Absorb that for a moment, 23 percent of Americans polled did not believe that the President was born in the United States. When broken down along party lines, 93 percent of Democrats, 83 percent of Independents and 42 percent of Republicans believe Barack Obama was born in the country. That meant that 58 percent of respondents polled who self-identified as Republicans did not believe that their commander-in-chief was a natural-born citizen.

When this poll drilled down to the regional level, the true nature of these sentiments came through. In the northeast 93 percent, Midwest 90 percent and west 87 percent felt that Obama was born in the United States. The south responded with 47 percent believing that our current President was born in Hawaii. Given those prior responses, it meant that most of the national no and not-sure responses were southern Republicans. If you map where the Jim Crow laws were most prevalent it seems to establish at least a subjective relationship.

When viewing a map of the United States that illustrates the 2008 presidential election results it was not difficult to determine where more than mere issues played a role in the outcome.

The state of Hawaii had twice issued statements that the birth certificate of Barack Obama was authentic. After Obama was born there were two separate birth announcements published in local newspapers. The real truth of the "Birther" backlash against the President was uglier than many wanted to talk about in public view. The mischaracterization of President Obama as some kind of foreigner elected to carry out a secret master plan allowed some to easily mock the President with disrespectful signs and depictions. It became commonplace to see posters proudly displayed with President Obama shown with a Hitler like appearance. Disrespectful acts that disparaged President Obama were carried out without a hint of shame which illustrated the psychology of the people involved. Their concern was to prove allegiance to their cause over everything else. The lack of respect for President Obama was considered an understandable expression of their true feelings. The idea of television cameras broadcasting individuals engaged in displaying inflammatory posters seemed to be of little concern to the people involved.

The next chapter will look at who elected Barack Obama and why that left a "mean middle" that staunchly opposed the President of the United States.

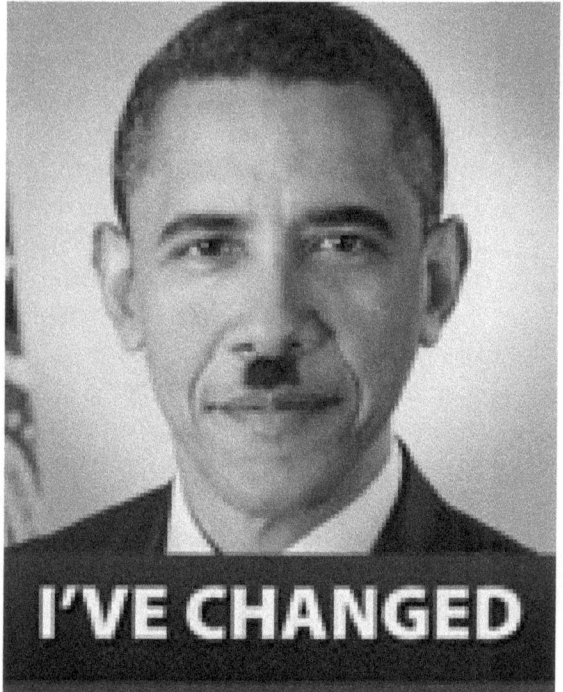

Obama depicted-as-Hitler poster
that health-care reform protesters
displayed at health-care town-hall
meetings.

Chapter 7

♦

The ugly core of distrust of President Obama
was at its essence centered on the historical
social position of the black man in American
society. Barack Obama was called the first
post-racial presidential candidate. For a
substantial number of the almost seventy
million people who voted for Obama, he was
judged beyond his race. Some of the near
sixty million citizens that voted against
Barack Obama, although many would not
admit it, did so with race as a major factor.
According to Pew Research exit polling
published on November 12, 2008, one of the
few groups that voted for McCain over
Obama were whites over thirty years old.
White voters over thirty went for McCain by

a margin of 57 percent to 41 percent. That age split in racial perception of the same candidate was destined to leave a bitter taste in the mouths of Obama's opponents. A portion of the voters who came out on the losing end of the 2008 election were not going to simply accept the new President as their own and line up behind him. The effort to discredit Barack Obama would continue almost unfazed by the actual election results. Many who voted against him just did not trust Obama.

The distrust of the new President was not a strictly southern states issue, but seemed to fit a profile of white voters who were older as well as those who lived in more rural areas. The south was concentrated with people more disposed to oppose President Obama in general. Some long-dormant racial feelings were inflamed during the long campaign season.

Many of the old Jim Crow laws dealt with the restrictions placed upon intimate relationships between whites and minorities. Given the history of murder and violence against black males for actual or perceived advances towards white women, it was easy to understand the charged atmosphere of exchanges between Barack Obama and Hillary Clinton. Every comment from Obama that could be seen as remotely condescending elicited a sharp response from the media. Obama said to Hillary Clinton, "You're likable enough Hillary," during one of their debates and was accused of being derisive.

When presidential candidate Obama was touring a manufacturing plant he referred to a female reporter as "sweetie" when telling her that he could not answer her question, but a press avail would take place later. The Senator later called the reporter with an apology. That was when I realized the tightrope Barack Obama had to walk when dealing with Caucasian women under a worldwide microscope. As it turned out the biggest potential pitfall was yet to come and she would roll in from Alaska full of historical and symbolic baggage.

When John McCain selected Sarah Palin as his running mate for the general election it sent shockwaves through the political landscape. I think Republican strategists saw her as anti-Obama kryptonite.

Sarah Palin fit a certain mold that would appeal to the core of the right-wing of the Republican Party. She held staunchly conservative views. Palin was an anti-abortion, abstinence only, gun advocate wrapped inside an attractive package. Her husband and five children cemented her family-first credentials. She presented an acceptable alternative to juxtaposition against Barack Obama and his equally appealing family for totally different reasons.

Sarah Palin was also in a strange way a balancing factor for John McCain. McCain was a war hero, but his age and affluence through his wife did not make him exactly one of the common people. The stories about his multiple homes became cannon fodder and were used to paint him as an elitist. Sarah Palin seemed to be a state-governing, child-raising and moose-hunting superwoman.

Sarah Palin took the stage at the Republican National Convention and set the place on fire with a scorching brand of mocking sarcasm directed towards the Democratic Party presidential Nominee Barack Obama. It was really a stunning moment to see someone that was a virtual unknown on the national political stage attacking the Democratic standard bearer for President of the United States.

Comparisons were drawn between Palin's experience and Obama's. That was done in order to try and elevate her to a level that made her seemed to be as viable of a candidate to be President, if necessary, as Barack Obama. It became a game of belittle the community organizer in order to elevate the small town mayor and Alaska Governor.

It was how Sarah Palin, with an unconventional speaking style, executed the role of political attack dog that took many by surprise. Her opening lines attacking the validity of a community organizer like Barack Obama rising to the level of candidate for President of the United States was just an initial salvo. Her rhetoric would slowly ratchet up from Obama's functional credentials to questioning his core values as an American.

Palin became the cult leader of the so called "Real Americans. As best as I could determine, Palin and the right-wing Republican definition of "Real Americans" had to do with geography, education level and race. I'll delve into the Real American issue later when we look into what I term the new "code" language that cropped up during the presidential election of 2008.

Sarah Palin cut a figure that was most incongruous given the words that were spewing forth from her mouth. Standing behind a podium dressed in fashion-high-heeled pumps, expensive clothing and a Hollywood cosmetics treatment, she became an icon to conservative working class white Americans. Her general appeal would continue to narrow as her background and views became better known. Palin was not only the anti-Barack Obama, she was also the anti-Hillary Clinton.

It soon became apparent that the only thing Palin had in common with Clinton was gender. The fact that Sarah Palin was a woman was not going to be enough to convince the legion of Clinton supporters to vote Republican over Barack Obama. Sarah Palin's views were the polar opposite of Hillary Clinton's on many issues including those concerning a woman's rights to choose abortion. The selection of Sarah Palin in regards to Hillary Clinton's women supporters was a Republican bet that a combination of gender and racial preference would overcome ideology. In the end Palin did not swing the Clinton voters over to John McCain. McCain in many ways became the side show to his running mate. Palin's rallies would often outdraw his events. McCain often campaigned with her and many would leave after she spoke instead of waiting to hear what the top of the Republican ticket had to say.

Sarah Palin reminded me of someone firing up a lynch mob. Phrases like "Palling around with a domestic terrorist" and "sounds like socialism to me" became her stock and trade when referring to Barack Obama. The audiences that she was drawing became increasingly strident in their negative tone towards Obama. Shouts of kill him, traitor and terrorist were caught on microphones covering the events. The seminal moment came in October of 2008, when McCain himself had to talk a woman down at a rally in Minnesota who approached him and said about Obama, "I can't trust Obama. I have read about him and he's not, he's not uh — he's an Arab. He's not — "John McCain cut her off and replied, "No, ma'am. He's a decent family man, citizen that I just happen to have disagreements with on fundamental issues and that's what this campaign's all about."

Sarah Palin's runaway train had largely derailed a few weeks before the November 5 election. One entanglement after another continued to spill forth from an abuse-of-power scandal involving her Alaskan state trooper ex-brother-in-law, unmarried pregnant teen-aged daughter to a campaign clothing purchase scandal. With disastrous network television interviews added in with other issues, Sarah Palin fizzled out. It was to the point that some Republicans called for her to withdraw from the ticket in favor of a last-minute replacement.

Given all of the turmoil, distractions and arrows flung in his direction, Obama resisted the trap of hitting back at Palin which surely would have created a media backlash of huge proportions. Joe Biden even managed to avoid any major pitfalls during a Vice-Presidential debate in which Governor Palin winked her eye into the camera at the entire United States.

Let us not mince words here. Sarah Palin would have not been taken seriously if she was anyone else. The woman could barely put together a coherent paragraph and could not name any newspapers that she read when asked. Sarah Palin was all about playing cultural and racial politics and it failed. The problem was many of the people that subscribed to her brand of hate speech took it to heart and the fruit of that was an ongoing bitter harvest. The losing team had gone away. McCain went back to the Senate and Palin abruptly quit her post as governor of Alaska. Their faithful followers were left to writhe in the agony of having someone they viewed as a possible socialist and terrorist sympathizer who was not a valid United States citizen as President.

Sarah Palin made news again on August 8, 2009, with a posting on the social networking site, Facebook, stating that Obama's health-care plan would include a "death panel" that would deny care to the neediest Americans. Palin was repeating something that a health-care executive came up with, but coming from her introduced it to a broader audience. The beat goes on.

Chapter 8

♦

When Barack Obama was born in Hawaii in 1961, blacks and whites had separate areas in bus terminals throughout the south. The freedom riders were undergoing brutal treatment as they rode buses throughout the south during 1961. One incident involved the stoppage of a busload of riders who were allowed to be beaten by the Ku Klux Clan for 15 minutes while the police watched. This was not exactly the ideal environment for a child who would be considered black to become President of the United States within fifty years.

A generation in the United States is approximately twenty-five years. Social behaviors are passed on from one generation to the next. Would slightly less than two generations from the legislative end of Jim Crow laws with the enactment of the voting rights act in 1965 be enough passage of time to elect a black President? Part of the answer was contained in how long some areas would cling to segregated practices beyond the legal end of the separated races laws.

In 1965 I went to public school for the first time and attended an all black elementary school that was farther away from my home than the white elementary school. In 1966 students had a choice of going to the black school or formerly all white school. In 1967 the black schools were shuttered and all students went to the same schools. It was definitely a period of adjustment. On April 4, 1968, Martin Luther King, Jr. was assassinated. I was in the third grade and frankly my memory of the event is a blur. I visited the scene of the crime as an adult many years later with my family.

The **Civil Rights Act of 1964** outlawed racial segregation in schools, public places and employment. It legally ended Jim Crow laws in the United States. The Voting Rights Act of 1965 outlawed discriminatory voting practices such as literacy tests designed to disenfranchise minority voters. Even after those pieces of legislation were passed, four states still imposed poll taxes until declared unconstitutional in 1966 by the federal courts. Those final states were Texas, Alabama, Virginia and Mississippi.

In a strange personal twist, I attended an integrated elementary school in 1967, but black citizens in our community continued to exclusively frequent the traditionally all-black public park. I clearly recall going to the previously blacks-only park as late as 1975. I may have been a victim of Jim Crow conditioning that required a long passage of time to overcome. I never knew if this was by rule or choice as the larger facility that was formerly only for white citizens was on the opposite side of town. Initially separation of the races in social situations was simply the norm. As integration took hold, my world gradually changed to a new normal but it was not as easy as flipping a switch.

In what seemed like a time warp, a documentary made by Canadian filmmaker Paul Saltzman chronicled a small town in Mississippi that held its first integrated High School prom in 2008. The students of the high school in Charleston, Mississippi held separate privately funded white and black proms until 2008. I think this should give you a flavor of how ingrained racial attitudes born by years of oppressive segregation and subjugation could become. Just to emphasize the point, the following page contains a map of the states that Obama and McCain won on election night.

2008 Presidential Election Map

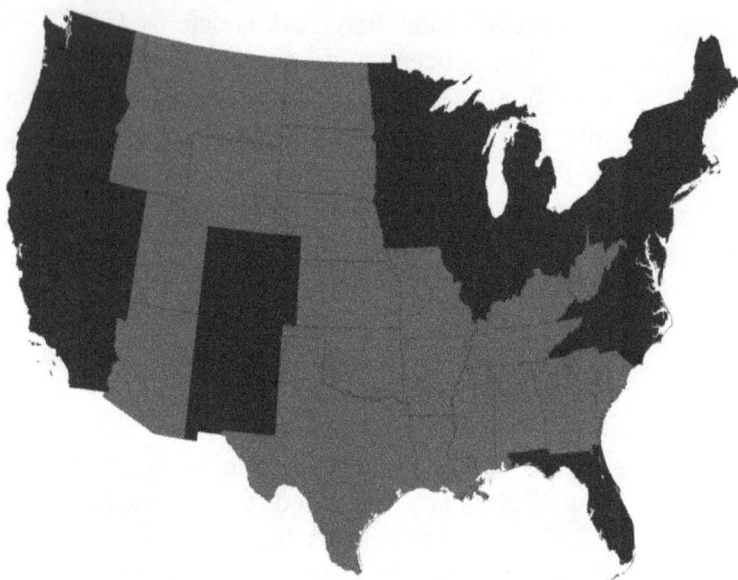

Obama

McCain

The near wipeout of Obama in the Deep South and middle of the country comprise what I describe as the "mean middle." Obama gathered a sizable amount of votes in the states that he lost, but some of those who voted against him harbored more than a casual dislike for the Democratic Party candidate. To crystallize that assertion was a point made by Jonathan Tilove in an article he wrote for The Times-Picayune newspaper November 8, 2008. Tilove wrote:

"However, while Obama was improving on Kerry's performance in most states -- including such critical battlegrounds as Pennsylvania, Ohio, Michigan, Indiana and North Carolina -- he did worse than Kerry among white voters in a handful of states -- especially Alabama, Mississippi and Louisiana.

In Louisiana, Obama's support among white voters was 10 percentage points below what Kerry received. That was the sharpest decline in white support for the Democratic ticket from 2004 to 2008 recorded in any state."

The white voting pattern in the Deep South was moving in a direction that went against the flow of the rest of the country. The result of what took place on election night in 2008 was not just a group that lost an election, but a group that was deeply dissatisfied with the elected leader of the country. That is why efforts to paint Barack Obama as a socialist, terrorist, illegal alien and any other figure worthy of disdain gained so much traction. Many of the people who did not vote for him felt a sense of vindication when doubts about Obama's validity to be President arose. Some of those people had a bitter taste in their mouths about someone whom they felt was inferior to them, by virtue of the blood coursing through his veins, being the commander-in-chief. Feelings such as those were not easily overcome because they were culturally ingrained.

The news was not all grim as younger white voters broke form on a nationwide basis and voted for Obama in larger numbers than those over thirty years old. It seemed that integration bore some fruit as it was more difficult to mischaracterize a group of people that were familiar due to daily interactions.

Obama won three traditionally southern states that had changed due to influxes of new residents over the years. The bottom line was that Barack Obama won the general election by nine and one-half million votes and amassed over 192 more electoral votes than John McCain. Obama would still be President even if he had lost all of the southern states.

Something else occurred during the presidential campaign of 2008. A new code language developed that not only drew racial lines, but cultural and educational distinctions as well.

Chapter 9

♦

Racial code language has long existed in the
United States. Something quite interesting
transpired during the campaign leading up to
the 2008 presidential election. The culturally-
conservative wing of the Republican Party
defined fresh lines of division and added new
terms to the lexicon.

One disturbing occurrence of the
presidential campaign was a purging of
intellectualism from the ranks of the
Republican Party. Many moderate
Republicans left of their own accord and the
messages going out on the campaign trail
appealed more to the basest cultural and
social elements of the party.

The term "Real Americans" became a
divisive term that was used often to draw

distinctions between those who lived in rural areas and urban dwellers. That same term also had an educational level element and racial undertones. Sarah Palin was a master at throwing around the term "Real Americans", but even she went too far when she once said that some areas of the country were more pro-America than others. Her assertion was that small towns were more pro-America than large cities. Palin later apologized for her remarks.

As best as I could determine, "Real Americans" were white, liked to hunt, fish, lived in rural areas and were not highly educated. Of course the driving force behind the "Real Americans" movement was the fact that Barack Obama was running for President. To prove how potent the "Real Americans" tag was as a flashpoint was the blowback a cable news co-anchor received when she indicated that Sarah Palin supporters were "Real Americans" as gauged by the size of the crowds she drew when the campaign was underway. The angry emails began to pour in immediately. This occurred during the summer of 2009 after Palin had resigned as Governor of Alaska. Americans did not take it lightly when they were told that somehow who you were, where you lived or your level of education made you more or less genuine than someone else.

Another small flare up was the American-flag lapel pin controversy. Critics railed against Barack Obama for not wearing an American-flag lapel pin and raised questions about his patriotism. Often those leveling criticism were not wearing American-flag lapel pins themselves. The idea of symbolic patriotism that you could put on by wearing an American-flag lapel pin that may have been made in China was quite an odd concept. In truth, it was patriotism at the most shallow level of visual identification.

Other terms became slurs that indicted cities, states and institutions. The city of San Francisco became a most reviled term when candidate Obama made a remark about people being bitter and clinging to their guns and religion. This remark was recorded during a fund raiser in San Francisco. Hillary Clinton used the "bitter" comment and clubbed Obama about the head in rural areas of Pennsylvania during the Democratic Party primary and it continued into the general election. San Francisco was also tied to the Speaker of the House, Nancy Pelosi, who was the favorite liberal target for conservatives. Obama with his Harvard-Law-School education was painted as an elitist. The very idea that a black man, who was largely raised by his grandparents, was an elitist should have been laughable. If there was ever an all-American story of someone pulling themselves up by his bootstraps, it should have been Barack Obama. There was only one problem. Obama did not come out of central casting. He was not the right type for many to line up behind.

What are we to make of terms such as "latte sipping liberals" or the "faculty lounge set"? Those terms are very dangerous because they draw a circle that excludes education as well as play to classism. At the heart of the divisiveness involved in the class-warfare politics that was played out, was an implication that those accepting the message assumed a view of inferiority from others. In its most cynical form, the message was to avoid the traits that defined the targets of their ridicule, such as seeking higher education. Could this group really revel in telling their supporters that elevating their station in life through the time-honored tradition of going to college was not a desirable thing to do? At the end of the celebration of Joe and Jane Six Pack and elevation of Joe the Plumber to iconic status, reality set in. John McCain went back to the Senate and his multiple homes. Sarah Palin went back to Alaska and was then poised to cash in on millions of dollars in book, speaking and media opportunities. Left behind were those who chanted, shouted and truly believed that they were in the presence of kindred souls. The faithful were abandoned to cling to emotions that were inflamed in the name of political gain.

As a summary some of the new code language included:

Real American – A term used to draw distinctions between conservative rural white voters and voters in urban areas. The term also had ethnic and class connotations attached to how it was used.

Elitist – This word was used to great effect to paint candidate Obama as someone who had personal tastes above that of the average American voter. Obama made a comment about the price of Arugula to farmers in Iowa and it was used to paint him as an elitist. I feel this word will be used as a substitute for the less acceptable "uppity" to refer to educated and well heeled black people.

Faculty Lounge – A term used to denigrate academics and highly educated individuals and paint them as out of touch with the real world and "Real Americans

San Francisco Liberal – A term used to paint someone as having very liberal views to the point of fanaticism and irrationality.

Articulate – A reverse slur. Saying a black person was very articulate meant that it was an anomaly for that ethnic group.

Good Speaker – Praising one aspect of an individual's ability while implying an inability to actually perform the required task beyond talking about it. That term was often used when referring to an African American who has laudable oratory abilities.

One of us – This phrase literally states that if you are of a different background, have different tastes or a different race, you are not one of us

Hard-working Americans – This term implies that certain Americans worked harder than others by default. This phrase appealed to individuals who thought other individuals or groups were getting a free ride that they, as hard-working Americans, were paying for.

Take my country back – This was a very pointed phrase that appealed to individuals who felt "others" had taken over the country. With a black President it was even more potent. Some of the groups that a number of people felt had taken their country were liberals, illegal immigrants, minorities, gays and intellectuals.

Hockey moms – There was something about the term hockey moms that appealed to a certain group and excluded other groups. Introduced by Sarah Palin at the 2008 Republican National Convention, the term may have literally meant that she was a hockey mom. As it was used on the campaign trail it seemed to mean a certain type of mom who was probably rural and white.

Family values – The speaker shaped this normally benign phrase. Conservatives co-opted the term to represent a set of conservative beliefs as opposed to reality. The use of the term generally meant anti-abortion, possibly abstinence-only stance, anti-gay, Christian, conservative political stance, etc.

The term also inferred that those values existed more in certain areas of the country than others. Often the individuals espousing the family values message have found themselves embroiled in family embarrassments ranging from unwed teenage pregnancy, marital infidelity and prostitution entanglements.

Latte Sipping Liberal – This referred to individuals who supported liberal issues and implied while they supported some causes of the less fortunate, they were completely out of touch with the real needs of regular people. The term suggested that some people that supported Obama lived in a comfortable cocoon and were disconnected from real America.

Exotic – Conservative Republican Pat Buchanan used this particularly derogatory term to describe Barack Obama on June 16, 2008, on the former MSNBC news show Verdict. Buchanan said that the term referred to how Obama talked one way to people in Pennsylvania face-to-face, but talked about them another way to donors in San Francisco. The term Exotic is used in America to refer to people from other cultures, such as Asian, where we have little general knowledge of their customs. Exotic is also used when referring to unusual pets such as pythons or rare breeds of dogs. Exotic also refers to custom hybrid breeds of animals such as dogs, cats and cattle. The word exotic could have been an inference towards Obama's bi-racial heritage, Hawaiian upbringing and period of living in Indonesia as a child. It seemed to be a feeble attempt to tag Obama as strange and foreign, but other guests on the program that day pushed back vigorously and the label did not stick.

The interesting thing about the new code language was that race was a subset swept up inside class, geography and political orientation.

Chapter 10

♦

What would be the next turn of the crank in this incredible journey of the soul of America? There have been two group efforts of dubious origins that opposed efforts of the President. One of these efforts was called "Tea Bag Parties" and the stated purpose was to protest escalating spending in Washington. Those gatherings started on tax day, April 15, 2009. The tone of those protests was decidedly right wing and much of the venom was aimed towards President Obama. In fact Rick Perry the governor of Texas suggested that his state could secede from the union but saw no reason to do it. After making those statements, the governor made himself and the state of Texas the butt of jokes on late-night comedy television programs for several days.

There were strong suspicions that the tea bag parties were less than true grass-roots efforts and sponsored by certain media interests. The term attached to the tea bag parties and some other protests to follow was Astroturf, which refered to an early form of artificial turf that was used on football fields.

Mark Knoller is a White House Correspondent for CBS News and he posted the following on the CBS News website on September 29, 2008:

"With no fanfare and little notice, the national debt has grown by more than $4 trillion during George W. Bush's presidency."

"It's the biggest increase under any president in U.S history."

"On the day President Bush took office, the national debt stood at $5.727 trillion. The latest number from the Treasury Department shows the national debt now stands at more than $9.849 trillion. That's a 71.9 percent increase on Mr. Bush's watch."

Given the above information and the original $700 billion bailout that President Bush signed in October 2008, why did the tea bag parties only start after President Obama took office? It would seem that the unprecedented level of debt accumulated by the Bush administration would have spurred citizen protests of fiscal irresponsibility years ago. I say this with my tongue planted firmly in my cheek as I suspect other motivations drove the spontaneous citizen outrage that broke out on national tax day in 2009.

Reforming the broken national health-care system in the United States was a major cornerstone of Barack Obama's campaign. He wasted no time in pushing his national health-care agenda forward. The primary issue with the traditional private insurance health-care system was the over forty-million uninsured Americans. Many of the stated goals of the national plan seemed to be a slam dunk for the public. Insurance companies would no longer be able to deny coverage because of preexisting medical conditions. A public health-insurance option could offer a competitively priced government run program that would help keep private plans from steep price increases.

The current health-care system has at its center a payment system run by for-profit health insurance companies. These health insurance companies earn billions of dollars in profit that are paid to executives, drug companies and stockholders. Some of the profit margin earned by the insurance companies was created by medical care that was denied.

Earlier in this book I mentioned that Sarah Palin stated that the new national health-care plan would have a "death panel." If you think rationally about the current system, the exclusion of preexisting conditions is somewhat of a functional death panel depending on the nature of the excluded medical issue.

Congress went on recess during August of 2009 and members of Congress used that time to conduct town-hall meetings on the health-care reform effort. Loud, unruly and sometime physically aggressive groups of people turned up at various meetings shouting down the speakers, reciting the pledge of allegiance and one person dropped a gun at a gathering in Arizona.

Tuesday August 11, 2009, On Hardball with Chris Matthews on MSNBC, Matthews spoke with William Kostric, who brought a gun earlier that same day as he protested President Obama's health-care plan at a town-hall meeting in Portsmouth, New Hampshire.

Kostric wore a legal handgun that was strapped to his leg. He held a sign referencing this quote from Thomas Jefferson: "The tree of liberty must be refreshed from time to time, with the blood of patriots and tyrants."

Kostric said that carrying the gun was an expression of rights and not an expression of violence. Given this country's history of presidential assassination it does not require a rocket scientist to connect the dots on the symbolism of bringing a loaded gun to an event where the commander-in-chief would be in attendance.

At a later town-hall meeting in Arizona, multiple people arrived with AR-15 assault rifles outside of the meeting location. It was legal to carry the guns and one of the men with an assault rifle was black. Whether the individuals posed a real threat to the President or not, the casual nature of people carrying guns near presidential events was alarming. Four American Presidents have been killed in office by gunshots. Six American Presidents have survived assassination attempts by gun wielding assailants.

On August 13, 2009, multiple news sources reported that the Secret Service was investigating a man who reportedly held a sign reading "Death to Obama" while outside a health-care reform town-hall meeting in Maryland. The same sign also read, "Death to Michelle and her two stupid kids," referring to President Barack Obama's wife, stated local law enforcement authorities.

There are no lines to read between anymore. I get it. Some out there will never accept a black man as President of the United States. At the very least, respect the office if not the office holder.

What evolved during the health-care reform debate was a tactic as old as time.

Send in thugs to disrupt the party. The tactics employed by those groups shouting and sometimes shoving at town-hall meetings restricted the one thing they claimed to value, freedom. Free speech was being drowned out and one favorite tactic was to recite how we were on an expressway to socialism, communism or some other form of tyranny. One thing was clear and it was that the intent was to stop any progress at all. South Carolina Republican Senator Jim Demint said that stopping Obama on health-care could be his "Waterloo" and "break him." Those so-called grass roots revolts were about racism, money and politics.

The true danger of staged protests by groups armed with talking and shouting points are the naïve that get caught up in the fervor. When unknown wildcards are thrown into the mix, there is an added element of danger. Guns and knives were found at some of the meetings.

There was a rising tide of anger and Barack Obama was the easy target because he was the current President. Obama had the unfortunate circumstance of inheriting a crumbing palace that was stripped bare by the former occupants of the prior eight years. As he attempted to restore the nation to some semblance of stability and growth, he was absorbing the backlash from the prior two terms of mismanagement.

George W. Bush managed to get out of town just as his house of cards was falling in upon itself. On January 20, 2009, Barack Obama was a proud man and made history. Joy reverberated around the country and celebrations were many. The happiest man in Washington D C that day probably was not Obama, but Bush. The country was in an economic freefall and Bush had the luxury of letting the new guy clean up the mess he left behind and take the blame.

Even more shameful was the silence from Republican lawmakers who did little to nothing to calm the situation. Their silence concerning the bullying, lying and disrespect directed towards the President was tantamount to the police years ago standing by while the Klan beat freedom riders. What was their real unstated goal? Was it to light a fuse and claim innocence when everything exploded? Those in positions of power who opposed President Obama should have displayed the decency to urge civility and honesty from their supporters.

Chapter 11

♦

It is often stated that still waters run deep, but bigotry and racism run deeper. One of the fears of Barack Obama's presidency was his possibility of placing new Justices on the Supreme Court. That opportunity came quickly when in April 2009; Justice David Souter announced that he was retiring at the end of the court's term. A storm of speculation ensued over who the President would select to replace the outgoing justice.

Barack Obama selected Sonia Sotomayor, a judge on the U.S. Court of Appeals for the Second Circuit with Hispanic heritage. Both of judge Sotomayor's parents were from Puerto Rico and she was born and raised in The Bronx, New York. Given the reaction to Obama as President, many wondered what responses Sotomayor would receive. There would not be a long wait. Sotomayor, who had more experience on the bench than any sitting Supreme Court Justice at the time, was compared to a cleaning lady by a national conservative radio-talk-show host. Sotomayor was also called a racist and a reverse racist. The United States Senate confirmed Sotomayor on August 6, 2009, as an Associate Justice of the United States Supreme Court.

Barack Obama had left a large footprint on the United States in the space of eight months. The President signed the 819 billion dollar economic stimulus plan that came to his desk without a single Republican vote in favor of the measure. Chrysler and General Motors both went into and came out of bankruptcy with the leadership of the President as strategic moves to save the companies and millions of blue collar jobs. As a follow up, Obama created a program that removed older, fuel-inefficient cars from the road while rewarding consumers who purchased more fuel efficient new vehicles. The cash-for-clunkers program provided a jump start for automakers after a particularly rough period.

The most profound effect that Barack Obama had was on the face of the federal government. Positions of power such as Secretary of State, Attorney General,

Secretary of Homeland Security and Supreme Court Justice included women, African American and Latino American representation. If that reminds you of American society, then you would not be mistaken.

Not everyone was pleased to see members from demographic groups they would rather see in subservient positions wielding the immense power of the federal government. Women and ethnic minorities have held top positions in the federal government before, but that was never combined with the reality of an African-American President. Change is a process that has to be lived through before it becomes commonplace.

The previous status quo was not something that was going to change from the inside. Historically, people with power do not willingly relinquish their grasp on it. In the case of Obama, a crush of circumstances almost made the alternative choice foolhardy.

Amid the hateful speeches and chants coming from Republican campaign rallies, a tsunami of cold water rushed in when the economy crashed. Suddenly the hate speech seemed to fall flat as people instantly pivoted to the state of their retirement plans, jobs and futures. John McCain self-destructed by suspending his campaign with a failed stunt to save the economy. Barack Obama behaved rationally and displayed calm under pressure and that was a major reason he became President.

The question was, would rational voices in the Republican Party speak up and bring sanity to the toxic environment being created by extremists. My guess is they were afraid they did not have the ability to calm the mob. It would have been a strange position for national Republican leaders to be rebuffed by those they sought to control. If that occurred then the awkward position of limbo would have existed for leaders with a movement that left them behind. I truly felt elected Republicans had no control over the "Deathers", as many who spouted about Obama death panels that would kill grandma were called. On August 12, 2009, Republican Senator Charles Grassley from Iowa seemed to give validity to the death panel idea. Grassley was one of three Republican Senators working on a bipartisan health-care bill.

On August 23, 2009, Sam Stein wrote a piece in the Huffington Post on how Senator Grassley admitted that the health-care reform measures under consideration did not include death panels. Grassley made the admission on the CBS News program Face The Nation:

"I know the Pelosi bill doesn't intend to do that," said Grassley. "It won't do that," he added later.

It took almost two weeks of Grassley being pummeled by the media nationwide over why a respected Republican leader would feed the lunatic fringe of his party before he admitted the known facts. His explanation was that he was attempting to soothe the fears of agitated supporters at a town-hall meeting.

Chapter 12

♦

The primary reason so many who held the reigns of power, privilege and presumed superiority detested President Obama was that he represented an affront to their sensibilities. Barack Obama's father was a black man who came from Kenya and married a white woman from Kansas. To their union, Barack Obama was born. In the ultimate of ironies a black man whose blood line never passed through the crucible of American slavery became President of the United States.

In the old world of Jim Crow segregation, the marriage of the parents of the forty-fourth President of the United States would have been illegal. What did this mean to diehards who still believed that interracial relationships should not be allowed? Those who were mentally stuck in another time would never accept that a man of Obama's heritage was fit to be President. In their view only one profile was eligible to be the elected leader of the United States and that was a white male.

Barack Obama broke through on a number of fronts that had only been touched on before. Obama stifled much of the influence of big donors by generating a grass-roots movement of millions of regular citizens who donated small amounts to his campaign. That translated into a huge financial advantage over Hillary Clinton in the Democratic primary campaign and John McCain during the general election.

The use of social networking sites such as Myspace and Facebook allowed Obama to finally tap into young voters using mediums they could relate to. The fact that so many new voters entered the political landscape created another backlash. High voter participation is not necessarily the ultimate goal that some may think it is. Some on the right were actually suggesting that all of the new people energized by Barack Obama just did not understand the gravity of what they were involved in. The insinuation was that their lack of understanding would send the country down the wrong path for years. I guess we had circled back to the notion of a privileged voting class.

The efforts to stop Barack Obama during the long primary and short, although intense, general election sunk to new lows. One Republican advertisement tried to portray Obama as a sexual pervert because of a bill he supported when he was in the Illinois State Senate that recommended age-appropriate sex education. The aim of the bill was to instruct young children on how to protect themselves against child predators.

During the Democratic primaries an image of Obama, showing him dressed in traditional Somali tribal clothing during a 2006 Senate trip to Africa, was widely circulated. The intent was to spread suspicion that Obama was a Muslim.

Barack Obama made a trip to Germany after winning the Democratic nomination and gave a speech to a crowd estimated at 200,000 people. Promptly upon his return to the United States, the Republicans ran an ad characterizing Obama as a celebrity and compared him to Paris Hilton. Footage from Obama's speech was used as a backdrop for the advertisement. It was hard for me to recall an opponent's popularity being used as a negative. The intent was clearly to distance Barack Obama from "Real Americans" and paint him as an elitist.

Another distortion was the so-called refusal of Obama to place his hand over his heart during the Pledge of Allegiance at an event in Iowa. It turned out that it was the playing of the National Anthem and not the Pledge of Allegiance. Barack Obama stated that when he grew up he was taught to place his hand over his heart during the Pledge of Allegiance, but not during the National Anthem. This was an attempt to portray Obama as being less patriotic than other candidates.

Barack Obama had to withstand a barrage of advertising, political attacks and even one televised debate that could have been considered an ambush by the moderators. Nico Pitney conducted an analysis of four head-to-head debates between Barack Obama and Hillary Clinton and posted his results in the Huffington Post on April 20, 2008. Pitney's findings are listed below:

Barack Obama has received the overwhelming majority of scandal questions over the course of the four debates, by a margin of 17 to 4. Obama has fielded questions about his "bitter" remarks, his connections to 60s-era radical William Ayers, two questions about flag lapels, two questions about his alleged plagiarism of speeches, three questions on Louis Farrakhan, and eight about Jeremiah Wright.

Pitney's informal findings seemed to betray the popular myth that Barack Obama received a free ride from the media.

The United States is a great country and is often referred to as a melting pot. My contention is that America is a land of diversity that in many respects resembles a stew instead of soup. The reason that I use stew as an example is that the separate ingredients all contribute to the whole, but they still maintain their separate properties and unique flavor. Soup implies that the separate ingredients have melded together to create something completely different. We are not there yet.

Chapter 13

♦

Barack Obama is biracial because his father was black and his mother was white. Although his white heritage was clearly known, the media and people in general treated him as a black man with almost no regard to his Caucasian roots. That was a result of a hangover from the one-drop rule that basically stated if an individual had any trace of African blood, they were consider black.

Wikipedia.org stated the following:

The 1910–19 decade was the nadir of the Jim Crow era. Tennessee adopted a one-drop statute in 1910, and Louisiana soon followed. Then Texas and Arkansas in 1911,

Mississippi in 1917, North Carolina in 1923, Virginia in 1924, Alabama and Georgia in 1927, and Oklahoma in 1931. During this same period, Florida, Indiana, Kentucky, Maryland, Missouri, Nebraska, North Dakota, and Utah retained their old "blood fraction" statutes *de jure*, but amended these fractions (one-sixteenth, one-thirty second) to be equivalent to one-drop *de facto*.

Now you may say that this was all distant history. Before you proclaim the one-drop rule irrelevant, read the following from Wikipedia in 2009:

Walter Plecker of Virginia and Naomi Drake of Louisiana insisted on trying to label families of mixed ancestry as Black. In 1924, Plecker wrote, "Two races as materially divergent as the White and Negro, in morals, mental powers, and cultural fitness, cannot live in close contact without injury to the higher." A subtext to this concept was the assumption that Blacks were somehow "improved" through White intermixture.

When the U.S. Supreme Court outlawed Virginia's ban on inter-racial marriage in Loving v. Virginia (1967), it declared Plecker's Virginia Racial Integrity Act and the one-drop rule unconstitutional.

Despite this holding, the one-drop theory retains influence in U.S. society, from both sides of color lines.

Let us put the one-drop rule into proper perspective. In Virginia the one-drop rule was still law after the signing of the Civil Rights Act of 1964 and the Voting Rights Act of 1965. Six years after Barack Obama was born, the one-drop rule was still active law. That was why the political commentators were shocked to see Barack Obama win the State of Virginia in the 2008 election. What they would not say on national television is illustrated above.

A black man won the presidential election in a state that had a law on its books six years after he was born stating he was inferior due to his racial makeup. That was a shift that left some behind with their old thoughts, prejudices and frustrations. Some of those frustrations exploded in angry outbursts and created schizophrenic like social behavior patterns. Apparently two generations was not enough passage of time for some to accept someone once deemed genetically inferior by law as President.

As a black man it had never been an option before to support someone of my same race for President of the United States. It had always been normal for everyone except a white male to have someone of another race or gender holding the top office in the federal government. It was a new experience for millions of voters, to have someone so relatable running for President. I wondered if the feeling of involvement I had in 2008 was what others had always experienced. I could also understand the enthusiasm of women supporters of Hillary Clinton and Sarah Palin. Of course other black candidates had run for President before Obama, but they never captured any meaningful support from white voters that would give them a chance to capture the nomination of a major political party.

U.S. News and World Report published an article on February 15, 2008, that listed Shirley Chisholm, Lenora Fulani, Alan Keyes, Carol Moseley Braun, Al Sharpton and Jesse Jackson as black people who ran for President before Barack Obama.

EbonyJet.com published on January 12, 2009, that Fredrick Douglas received one vote from the Kentucky delegation at the 1888 Republican Convention in Chicago. That vote effectively made Fredrick Douglas the first black candidate nominated for United States President.

Barack Obama won the Presidency 120 years after Fredrick Douglas received the first vote nominating a black man to be commander-in-chief. Does the phrase, "The timing is not right yet," sound familiar?

One thing we have to remember is that the next time could be a long time coming.

Let us make the most of the current opportunity. Now that the impossible has occurred the opposition will not be docile again and will turn out to the polls in droves.

Chapter 14

♦

An event took place on Thursday July 16, 2009, in Cambridge Massachusetts, that exposed the still raw racial rift in America.

Krissah Thompson, a Washington Post Staff Writer, wrote on Tuesday, July 21, 2009:

"Henry Louis Gates Jr., one of the nation's most prominent African American scholars, was arrested last week at his home near Harvard University after trying to force open the locked front door."

According to the article, Gates who was fifty-eight years old and walked with a cane, was returning to his home from a trip to

China. When he tried to open the door to his house with his key, it was stuck and possibly tampered with. The driver who dropped Professor Gates off in front of his home came and assisted Gates in getting the door open.

While Gates and his driver were gaining entry to his house, a concerned neighbor called 911 and reported a possible incident of two people breaking into a house. The transcript of the 911 call was as follows:

911 OPERATOR: 9-1-1, what is the exact location of your emergency?

FEMALE WITNESS CALLER: Hi, I'm actually at (inaudible) street in Cambridge, the house number is 7 Ware Street.

911 OPERATOR: OK ma'am, your cell phone cut out, what's the address again?

FEMALE WITNESS CALLER: Sorry, it's 7 Ware Street. That's W-A-R-E Street.

911 OPERATOR: The emergency is at 7 Ware Street, right?

FEMALE WITNESS CALLER: Well no, I'm sorry. 17. Some other woman is talking next to me but it's 17, 1-7 Ware Street.

911 OPERATOR: What's the phone number you're calling me from?

FEMALE WITNESS CALLER: I'm calling you from my cell phone number.

911 OPERATOR: All right, tell me exactly what happened?

FEMALE WITNESS CALLER: Um, I don't know what's happening. I just had an older woman standing here and she had noticed two gentlemen trying to get in a house at that number, 17 Ware Street. And they kind of had to barge in and they broke the screen door and they finally got in. When I had looked, I went further, closer to the house a little bit after the gentlemen were already in the house. I noticed two suitcases. So, I'm not sure if this is two individuals who actually work there, I mean, who live there.

911 OPERATOR: You think they might have been breaking in?

FEMALE WITNESS CALLER: I don't know 'cause I have no idea. I just noticed.

911 OPERATOR: So you're saying you think the possibility might have been there? What do you mean by barged in? You mean they kicked the door in?

FEMALE WITNESS CALLER: No, they were pushing the door in. Like, umm, the screen part of the front door was kind of like cut.

911 OPERATOR: How did they open the door itself with the lock?

FEMALE WITNESS CALLER: They, I didn't see a key or anything 'cause I was a little bit away from the door. But I did notice that they pushed their (interrupted).

911 OPERATOR: And what do the suitcases have to do with anything?

FEMALE WITNESS CALLER: I don't know, I'm just saying that's what I saw.

911 OPERATOR: Do you know what apartment they broke into?

FEMALE WITNESS CALLER: No, they're just they first floor. I don't even think that it's an apartment. It's 17 Ware Street. It's a house, it's a yellow house. Number 17. I don't know if they live there and they just had a hard time with their key but I did notice that they kind of used their shoulder to kind of barge in and they got in. I don't know if they had a key or not because I couldn't see from my angle. But, you know, when I looked a little closely that's what I saw.

911 OPERATOR: (inaudible) guy or Hispanic?

FEMALE WITNESS CALLER: Umm.

911 OPERATOR: Are they still in the house?

FEMALE WITNESS CALLER: They're still in the house, I believe, yeah.

911 OPERATOR: Were they white, black or Hispanic?

FEMALE WITNESS CALLER: Umm, well there were two larger men, one looked kind of Hispanic but I'm not really sure. And the other one entered and I didn't see what he looked like at all. I just saw it from a distance and this older woman was worried thinking someone's breaking in someone's house, they've been barging in.

And she interrupted me and that's when I had noticed otherwise I probably wouldn't have noticed it at all, to be honest with you. So, I was just calling 'cause she was a concerned neighbor, I guess.

911 OPERATOR: OK, are you standing outside?

FEMALE WITNESS CALLER: I'm standing outside, yes.

911 OPERATOR: All right, the police are on the way, you can meet them when they get there. What's your name?

FEMALE WITNESS CALLER: Yeah, my name is (deleted).

911 OPERATOR: All right, we're on the way.

FEMALE WITNESS CALLER: Ok. All right, I guess I'll wait. Thanks.

After reading the transcript, two things stand out. The first thing that jumped out was the caller reported that there were two suitcases present and thought that maybe the two men could have lived there. The second item of note was that the caller never mentioned race until asked by the 911 operator.

Subsequent to the 911 call, the Cambridge police were dispatched and eventually Professor Henry Louis Gates Jr. was arrested, handcuff and driven away in custody from his own home. The charge was disorderly conduct, which was dropped but not before mug shots and images of a handcuffed Gates standing on the front porch of his home were circulated through news media sources nationwide.

The Cambridge, Massachusetts police department's incident report # 9005127 that was entered on 7/16/2009   stated:

When I arrived at 17 Ware Street I radioed ECC and asked that they have the caller meet me at the front door to this residence. I was told that the caller was already outside. As I was getting this information, I climbed the porch stairs toward the front door. As I reached the door, a female voice called out to me. I turned and looked in the direction of the voice and observed a white female, later identified as Lucia Whalen. Whalen, who was standing on the sidewalk in front of the residence, held a wireless telephone in her hand and told me that it was she who called. She went on to tell me that she observed what appeared to be two black males with backpacks on the porch of 17 Ware Street. She told me that her suspicions were aroused when she observed one of the men wedging his shoulder into the door as if he was trying to force entry. Since I was the only police officer on location and had my back to the front door as I spoke with her, I asked that she wait for other responding officers while I investigated further.

Whalen's attorney said her client never mentioned the race of the men to Officer Crowley. Whalen was upset by reports she thought unfairly portrayed her as a racist.

Lucia Whalen was the female witness caller who made the 911 call reporting the incident.

This incident was a tailor-made trap for President Barack Obama, the first African-American Head-of-State. On Wednesday July 22, 2009, President Obama stepped directly onto the racial explosive at the end of a nationally televised press conference on health-care reform. Near the end of the news conference, Obama was asked about the Professor Gates arrest and he answered without hesitation:

"I don't know – not having been there and not seeing all the facts – what role race played in that, but I think it's fair to say, number one, any of us would be pretty angry; number two that the Cambridge police acted stupidly in arresting somebody when there was already proof that they were in their own home," Obama said in response to a question from the Chicago Sun-Times's reporter Lynn Sweet.

The President later added:

"Separate and apart from this incident is that there's a long history in this country of

African-American and Latinos being stopped by law enforcement disproportionately," the president said, eagerly engaging the issue of racial profiling, a concern earlier in his career that has seen little White House attention to date.

"That's just a fact," Obama said of profiling. "That doesn't lessen the incredible progress that has been made."

The response to what President Obama said was immediate, forceful and largely divided along racial lines. This story had many historically racial flashpoints. The relationship of the black community with the police has been long and troubled. The Rodney King beating in Los Angeles and the killing of Sean Bell in New York by three police officers on his wedding day with a fifty-bullet barrage are two infamous incidents. The three officers in the Bell incident were acquitted.

Obama admitted that he was a friend of Professor Gates when he answered the question put before him. What was curious in the response to the President's answer was how many portrayed it as an attack on law enforcement. Another strange reaction was the minimizing of the sanctity of an individual's rights when he is in his own home compared to the power of a law enforcement officer who enters that home.

The arrest of Gates was a perfect opportunity for those groups espousing that we "take our country back" to rally behind the professor and protest undue government intrusion on individual rights.

Another opportunity missed was by those fearing that we will become a socialist country. Many of our services that we take for granted are in fact a form of socialism. Police departments, fire departments, public highways, Social Security and Medicare fall into the category of socialist style undertakings because they are tax supported for the common good of everyone they serve.

Sarah Palin should have been on the first flight to Boston when she heard about Professor Gate's arrest by the Cambridge police in his home. She should have been standing on Gates front porch protesting the intrusion of the police into the home of an American citizen and arresting him. Why do you imagine that the responses from those on the right who shouted about individual freedoms were squarely behind the police who seemed to be standing on shaky ground? The answer is the profile of the victim did not fit their narrative. In some circles the black Harvard Professor fits the mold of the "not-so-real Americans" as define during the 2008 presidential campaign.

If roles were reversed and a distinguished white professor was arrested under the same circumstances by a black police officer, I think the reaction would have been totally reversed. The focus from right-wing conservatives was that Gates shot his mouth off to a cop and deserved what he got. Black Americans focused on the fact that the man was in his own home and when the officer confirmed that no crime was committed, he should have left the scene.

President Obama backed the professor, who happened to be black, and was accused of racism against a white police officer. In fact this incident was used in a failed attempt to paint the President as favoring blacks over whites. It was quickly pointed out that many of the key members of the White House inner circle were white. The assertion that Obama was a racist fell flat and many could say that it boomeranged on his accusers.

What was noticeable to keen observers was the tepid treatment that the media gave to the inconsistent accounts of Gates arrest contained in the police report compared to what the 911 caller stated.

The fact that President Barack Obama did not hesitate in giving his response to a loaded question on a hot issue boosted his credibility among some doubters. The President's supporters wasted no time in facing down critics eager to fan the flames of this incident into a racial wildfire.

Barack Obama demonstrated his deft political touch again by calming the matter.

After making a couple of telephone calls he shared a few beers with the parties involved on the White House lawn accompanied by Vice President Joe Biden. What could have been a runaway racial wildfire was extinguished quietly while sitting around a table sharing beer and peanuts.

Chapter 15

♦

The summer of 2009 was long and hot in many ways. A black man named Barack Obama was President of the United States and embers of racial discord were flaring up across the country. Due to the dire straits of the nation's economy many of the incidents did not get the national attention they warranted.

A death that reminded me of the dragging death of James Byrd Jr. behind a pickup truck in Jasper, Texas in 1999, caused a racial standoff 10 years later in 2009. This incident occurred in the town of Paris, Texas.

Anna M. Tinsley of McClatchy Newspapers wrote in the Fort Worth Star Telegram on Wednesday July 29, 2009 :

But the Fort Worth activist with the Tarrant County Local Organizing Committee was in the national spotlight last week, helping lead a protest against alleged racial injustice in Paris, Texas.

"There is still a great deal of racism and injustice in this country, even though we have a black president," Blackwell said. "People think racism has gone away, but that is not true."

The Paris case, in which charges were dropped against two white men who had been accused of running over and dragging their black friend last year, is one of several recent racial incidents generating headlines.

The rally in Paris concerned the death of 24-year-old Brandon McClelland, whose body was found September 16, 2008, on a country road.

Initially, two of McClelland's white friends were charged with his murder. Those charges were dropped later due to a lack of evidence. Someone else came forward and said that he may have accidentally hit McClelland with his vehicle.

The death of McClelland occurred during 2008. That was one of those incidents that stood in such stark contrast with the election of Barack Obama that they seemed to be happening in different eras.

Another occurrence in Philadelphia, Pennsylvania that illustrated that region nor age is exempt from racism is this account of a group of children who were turned away from a swimming pool. Karen Araiza reported on Wed, Jul 29, 2009, and posted on the nbcPhiladelphia.com website:

"More than 60 campers from Northeast Philadelphia were turned away from a private swim club and left to wonder if their race was the reason.

"I heard this lady, she was like, 'Uh, what are all these black kids doing here?' She's like, 'I'm scared they might do something to my child,'" said camper Dymire Baylor.

The Creative Steps Day Camp paid more than $1900 to The Valley Swim Club. The Valley Swim Club is a private club that advertises open membership. But the campers' first visit to the pool suggested otherwise.

"When the minority children got in the pool all of the Caucasian children immediately exited the pool," Horace Gibson, parent of a day camp child, wrote in an email. "The pool attendants came and told the black children that they did not allow minorities in the club and needed the children to leave immediately."

The next day the club told the camp director that the camp's membership was being suspended and their money would be refunded."

The prior incidents were just two of numerous examples of a still toxic environment when it came to racial relations. Occasionally, one of those events will occur in a familiar area. I remember the following situation when it happened and found the story a little hard to believe. This account from Martha Deller of the Fort Worth Star Telegram recounted the trial:

"FORT WORTH — Three mental-health experts testified this week that a 67-year-old Arlington woman was legally insane when she bashed a neighbor in the face with a two-by-four after shouting racial slurs and threats at her.

On Friday, a Tarrant County jury rejected that defense and convicted Grace Head of misdemeanor assault in the Dec. 19, 2007, attack on Kay "Silk" Littlejohn in the yard of her Arlington home.

Jurors also convicted Head of misdemeanor criminal mischief for jumping onto the hood of Littlejohn's Toyota Camry, stomping the car and hitting its hood and roof with a stick.

They ruled that Head, who is white, targeted Littlejohn, who is black, because of her race. That finding elevates the two misdemeanors to state jail felonies with a maximum punishment of two years in jail.

The idea that a woman of the age of sixty-seven years old would attack her female neighbor with a two-inch by four-inch piece of lumber is incredible. The idea that she attacked her neighbor because she was black is simply sad.

The prior examples illustrated there was a huge gap between the millions who voted in good faith for Obama or McCain on issues versus that group who voted against Obama because they simply could not stomach the idea of a black man as their President. Many of the later group were feeling aggrieved and some took it out on others. It would be interesting to know how many of the vocal Obama opponents actually voted in the 2008 election at all. While many who saw their side lose decided to make the best of the situation and support President Obama for the good of the country, some felt wounded and betrayed.

Something else was at play in how some of these outbreaks of racism were cropping up nationwide. As in anything else, only a fraction of what was taking place actually reached a level that attracted media attention. It was those unknown slights because of skin color that may have caused the most damage. Someone out there was probably suffering in silence. Oddly enough there was another backlash that had emerged and that was the use of the often repeated reverse racism charge. Both Barack Obama and Supreme Court Justice Sonia Sotomayor were called racists. Peter Drivas of the Huffington Post wrote on August 6, 2009:

Fox News' Glenn Beck felt the consequences of his controversial comments on the July 28 episode of the Fox News morning show "Fox and Friends," when he said that Barack Obama was a "racist" who had a "deep-seated hatred for white people or the white culture."

Several major advertisers pulled their ads from Beck's television program that aired on Fox News. Beck is a popular conservative radio and television talk-show host with millions of loyal followers.

Chapter 16

♦

First Timothy 6:10 of the New International Bible states, "For the love of **money** is a root of all kinds of **evil**. Some people, eager for **money**, have wandered from the faith and pierced themselves with many griefs."

President Barack Obama had angered the money changers that preyed on the American public. The literal dealers in death panels marshaled their forces against him and employed base and vile tactics. The United States was the only modern industrial power without health-care coverage for all of its citizens. Our nation had a health-care system run by huge for-profit corporations whose charters were to increase value to the shareholders and executives.

We have literally witnessed on our television screens images of patients dying from neglect while inside the waiting areas of hospital emergency rooms. The tragedy of a health-care system with a profit motive involved means that there is a connection between profit, pain and death. One man's death could be another mans dividend.

Barack Obama recognized the tragedy and suffering of the forty-million-plus people in this country without health-care coverage and was elected to do something about it. Little did he realize the severity of the backlash as he attempted to turn words into action. The health insurance and pharmaceutical business is very lucrative with billions of dollars in profit. Executives that headed the health insurance companies garnered hundreds of millions of dollars in compensation. No one really knew what lengths they would go to in order to protect that financial empire. If destroying the first African-American President was the price of preserving the status quo, so be it.

It did not prove to be very difficult to recruit an anti-Obama army to attack the President. This was a simple case of the enemy of my enemy was my friend psychology. Barack Obama had divergent groups that wanted to see him fail. Republicans wanted to tear down Obama so that they could rebuild their rejected party and make gains during the next elections. Right-wing extremists despised the President because of his politics and race. Others were fighting Obama because reforming health-care would turn the spigot off on their health-insurance campaign funds. Birthers and Deathers joined together to place roadblocks in Obama's path.

The debate to stop President Obama on health-care reform took a strange personal turn and became hostile and racial. Accusations of the President being an illegal alien, Nazi and racist were shouted with impunity. Scenes that appeared to come from some movie about an alternative reality with protesters pushing, shoving and carrying guns flashed across our television screens. One altercation between a health-care reform supporter and a health-care reform opponent resulted in one of the men getting the tip of his pinky finger bitten off.

In order to understand what the health insurance industry was protecting, take a look at a report on executive compensation published May 20, 2009, by Michael Ricciardelli on healthreformwatch.com:

Ins. Co. & CEO With 2007 Total CEO Compensation

- Aetna- Ronald A. Williams: $23,045,834
- Cigna- H. Edward Hanway: $25,839,777
- Coventry Dale B. Wolf : $14,869,823
- Health Net Jay M. Gellert: $3,686,230
- Humana- Michael McCallister: $10,312,557

- U.Health Grp- Stephen J. Hemsley: $13,164,529
- WellPoint- Angela Braly (2007): $9,094,271
  L. Glasscock (2006): $23,886,169

Ins. Co. & CEO With 2008 Total CEO Compensation

- Aetna, Ronald A. Williams: $24,300,112
- Cigna, H. Edward Hanway: $12,236,740
- Coventry, Dale Wolf: $9,047,469
- Health Net, Jay Gellert: $4,425,355
- Humana, Michael McCallister: $4,764,309
- U. Health Group, Stephen J. Hemsley: $3,241,042
- Wellpoint, Angela Braly: $9,844,212

After reviewing the lucrative compensation listed above and considering others who were not listed, it is easy to understand what was being protected. What we must understand is the misery that the compensation and profits in the health insurance business is built upon. In any business profit is earned in one of two ways, either by selling more of your offering or controlling costs. The irony of health insurance companies is that they do not provide health care. Health insurance companies only pay for health care provided by doctors, hospitals and other medical care providers. Health-insurance firms decide who is covered, what is covered and what providers participate in the system. Every denial of coverage of medical care is more profit going to the bottom line of health insurance companies.

Barack Obama informed the nation of his mother's struggles as she was dying of cancer. He stated that she had to fight with insurance companies from her hospital bed to get coverage that she had already paid for as the companies tried to say that maybe it was a preexisting condition.

President Obama desired to free Americans from the issues that his mother faced in the midst of her illness. Obama wanted to remove hospital emergency rooms as the option of last resort for the masses of uninsured. The President wanted to ease the relentless squeeze of rising premiums and effects of medical costs driving families into financial ruin. The battle lines were draw and the battle enjoined.

The health-care reform fight provided cover for everyone else who wanted to take Obama down and it unleashed the dogs of hate.

Sam Stein of the Huffington Post posted on August 28, 2009:

Race-based attacks and criticism of President Obama have been on the rise during the dog days of August. And they're not just happening at health-care town-hall protests.

A reader sent over a picture of a group of protesters camped outside Rep. Susan Davis's (D-Calif.). "Neighborhood Day" event this past week, brandishing signs calling the President a Black Supremacist and suggesting he's a Nazi disciple.

The lengths elected politicians would go to as they joined in on the vile hate speech was truly shocking as pointed out later in the same article:

Earlier this week, Idaho Republican gubernatorial hopeful, Rex Rammell, said he'd buy a license to hunt Obama. Meanwhile, Rep. Lynn Jenkins, (R-Kans.) expressed her wish that the Republican Party would find a "great white hope" to take on the President in the next election.

Lynn Jenkins then went on to name several Republicans, who were all white, that she viewed as potential great white hopes to take on President Obama during the next presidential election. The term "great white hope" came about during the early 1900s when whites were attempting to find a champion to defeat the first black heavyweight champion, Jack Johnson. I assume Jenkins was indicating that the Republican Party needed a champion to defeat the black heavyweight presidential champion, but he needed to be white. Sorry Governor Jindal of Louisiana, Michael Steele and General Colin Powell, although all of you are Republicans, you need not apply.

Representative Lynn Jenkins later said that she meant a shining light and did not know the racial implications of her words and offered the "if anyone was offended apology." There was only one problem with her assertion of ignorance about the term "great white hope." Jonathon Cumberland posted information on the Daily Kos website on Friday Aug 28, 2009, information that totally debunks Lynn Jenkins' claims of innocence:

Jenkins, R-Kan., said Thursday **she didn't know "great white hope" had a negative connotation** when she recently used the phrase to describe Republicans' search for a new leader.

However, the freshman lawmaker **supported a resolution that included that exact phrase last month** when the House approved by unanimous consent a measure urging President Obama to pardon black U.S. boxer Jack Johnson. Johnson, who died in 1946, was the target of an early 1900s racist plot and convicted in 1913 of transporting a white woman across state lines for immoral reasons.

Within the resolution passed by the House July 29 was a passage that read,

"Whereas the victory by Jack Johnson over Tommy Burns prompted a search for a White boxer who could beat Jack Johnson, a recruitment effort that was dubbed the search for the 'great white hope."

Even more hypocritical was the fact that Representative Jenkins was from Kansas and her home town was thirty minutes from where the "great white hope" who defeated Jack Johnson, Jess Willard, lived. When Jack Johnson was imprisoned for transporting a white woman across state lines, he was housed in the United States Penitentiary in Leavenworth, Kansas. The prison where Johnson was incarcerated and the residence of the man that defeated him are in the district that Lynn Jenkins represents in Congress. Jenkins either has a horrible grasp of the history of the area she represents, had amnesia, did not know what she voted for or she meant what she said about finding a Republican "great white hope." Given her history she should know what the term meant better than anyone else.

There is something especially disrespectful when another elected politician or aspiring politician joined in attacking the President of the United States. What it clearly illustrated during candid moments when their true feelings burst through was how they actually felt about people different than themselves. The fact that a man who aspired to be a governor of a state in the union felt at ease saying that he would like to hunt the President like an animal was appalling. If there are no voices of reason on the right to quell the hateful rhetoric, we could be headed towards disaster.

Let us not be naïve. Almost seventy million Americans voted for Barack Obama and made him the forty-fourth President. They will not sit by in silence as the lunacy escalates.

History has proven that the norm of behavior is a shifting line when it was unopposed. As the protests became more outrageous and the signs became more disrespectful, we descended more into the abyss of our past. We are now reaping the harvest of distorted history.

Jason Linkins posted an excerpt of conservative Pat Buchanan's view of American history on July 17, 2009, in the Huffington Post. Buchanan was responding to a question from MSNBC host Rachel Maddow on why he thought that 108 of the 110 Supreme Court Justices had been white. He replied::

"White men were 100% of the people that wrote the Constitution, 100% of the people that signed the Declaration of Independence, 100% of the people who died at Gettysburg and Vicksburg, probably close to 100% of the people who died at Normandy. This has been a country built basically by white folks, who were 90% of the nation in 1960 when I was growing up and the other 10% were African-Americans who had been discriminated against. That's why."

Do not dismiss Buchanan's view as mindless ranting. The view that he expressed represented the way many thought in this country. People who held his point of view felt like someone else was taking something away that their ancestors built with their bare hands. Of course that view dismissed the efforts of everyone else in building this nation. Native Americans, African Americans, Women, Asian Americans, Hispanic Americans, Pacific Islanders and everyone else who had ever called themselves an American helped to build this country.

The view of Pat Buchanan was a narrow view through a selective lens of history. That lens had a filter that removed the effort and value of everyone else's contribution to our country's vitality. It was that filtered lens that allowed hate and contempt to flourish. That view enabled the President of the United States to be reduced to someone with no stake in the history of this nation. Obama's father did as many who traveled to America seeking opportunity. Barack Obama's maternal grandfather fought in World War II. The President's grandmother helped to build aircraft for the war effort during the Second World War. By any definition, Barack Obama's family embodied the definition of what building the country was all about.

The United States is the prototype of a nation built by immigrants and patriots. Barack Obama is a product of immigrants and patriots. Anyone that finds something lacking, have ulterior motives.

Chapter 17

♦

    While the election of Barack Obama as the first African America President was a cause for celebration, it was also a signal for vigilance. That vigilance was to be wary of efforts to undermine the future. Much of that undermining could come through our system of education.

    Two very loud signals went out from two Universities that invited President Obama to deliver commencement addresses at the beginning of his term.

    Arizona State University invited President Obama to deliver an address at their graduation but was declining to present him with the customary honorary doctorate degree. When questioned about why the school decided not to bestow the degree on the nations first black President, Al Kamen wrote in the Washington Post on April 9, 2009:

The reason given by university officials as to why the President was not getting the honorary degree was explained in an unusual way. It was said that the honorary degrees were bestowed upon individuals who has amassed a substantial body of work. President Obama was deemed to have not amassed a substantial enough of a body of work since his presidential term was just starting.

So becoming President of the United States, being a bestselling author and Grammy winner was not a substantial enough body of work to receive a honorary doctorate degree. That boggles the mind.

The very idea that a President of the United States was not accomplished enough to receive a traditionally issued doctorate degree was laughable. The firestorm of criticism that ensued caused much embarrassment for the university and promises from some donors to end their contributions in support of the institution. That episode was viewed as a supreme sign of disrespect for a man who broke through one of the toughest glass ceilings in history.

OBAMA GUILTY of BPWB   D T Pollard

President Obama's second brush with blowback from an educational institution was a furor over Notre Dame University's invitation to address their graduating class. The Pope and other Catholic leaders worldwide sent congratulations to President Obama without mention of his stance on abortion. The Los Angeles Times ran an editorial on April 1, 2009:

The same can't be said of conservative Catholics who are lobbying Notre Dame University, the best-known Catholic institution of higher learning in the country, to rescind an invitation to Obama to speak at its commencement in May and accept an honorary degree. Led by the Cardinal Newman Society, a self-appointed guardian of orthodoxy, the protesters seem to believe they were more Catholic than the Pope.

The argument against Obama's appearance at Notre Dame was that it's incompatible with the church's opposition to abortion and the use of embryonic stem cells in medical research. But a similar charge could have been leveled against the 2001 appearance at the University of George W. Bush, who as governor of Texas presided over scores of executions. Although the church's objections to the death penalty aren't as absolute as its opposition to abortion, U.S. bishops have taught since 1980 that "the legitimate purposes of punishment do not justify the imposition of the death penalty." For them, the death penalty is also a "life" issue.

Obama was singled out for special slights and rebukes, but he didn't allow those insults to bring him down to the level of his detractors. He delivered messages of hope to the graduates and lessons in humility to his detractors.

There was something else afoot that was receiving little attention. Through a quirk of consolidation, school books that are used in public schools nationwide are determined by what the state of Texas chooses for their curriculum. There was a request from some members of the body that decides the content included in the United States history text books to delete some figures and include others. An article posted July 14, 2009, in the Wall Street Journal online edition states:

Three reviewers, appointed by social conservatives, have recommended revamping the K-12 curriculum to emphasize the roles of the Bible, the Christian faith and the civic virtue of religion in the study of American history. Two of them want to remove or de-emphasize references to several historical figures who have become liberal icons, such as César Chávez and Thurgood Marshall.

Those types of changes shape the view that children have of themselves as they grow and mature. If they don't see how people who looked liked them helped build the nation, they may think less of their own worth and potential. Decisions that are made out of public view could have a profound effect on millions of children and their future.

On September 02, 2009, Mediamatters.org posted on its website a story about the reaction conservatives were having to a speech President Obama planned to deliver to the nation's school children. The subject of the speech was to encourage excellence and perseverance in educational pursuits. The speech was scheduled for September 8, 2009. Media Matters posted the following:

Numerous conservatives have claimed that President Obama's upcoming September 8 speech about "persisting and succeeding in school," along with classroom activities about the "importance of education," will "indoctrinate" and "brainwash" schoolchildren. Conservatives have compared Obama's address to Chinese communism and the Hitler Youth, while also calling for parents to "keep your kids home" from the "fascist in chief."

I think many students over the years have participated in assignments where they were told to watch the State of the Union speeches given by Presidents and write a report on it. President George H. W. Bush addressed school children with a "Just say no" message concerning drug use.

According to Wikipedia.org:

On the morning of September 11, 2001, George Bush was about to begin reading the story (The Pet Goat) along with a group of school children at Emma E. Booker Elementary School in Sarasota County, Florida when White House Chief of Staff Andrew Card informed him that an airplane had hit the World Trade Center. Bush remained seated and followed along as the children read the book, for over seven minutes.

One of the states with the loudest objections to President Obama speaking to their children over fears of indoctrination was Texas. Coincidentally Texas is requiring that the Bible be taught as a regular part of school curriculums in 2009. In order to quell fears of the President delivering some type of indoctrination to impressionable students, the White House released the prepared text of the speech on Labor Day September 7, 2009:

Prepared Remarks of President

Barack Obama
Back to School Event

Arlington, Virginia
September 8, 2009

The President: Hello everyone –
how's everybody doing today? I'm here with
students at Wakefield High School in
Arlington, Virginia. And we've got students
tuning in from all across America,
kindergarten through twelfth grade. I'm glad
you all could join us today.

I know that for many of you, today is
the first day of school. And for those of you in
kindergarten, or starting middle or high
school, it's your first day in a new school, so
it's understandable if you're a little nervous. I
imagine there are some seniors out there who
are feeling pretty good right now, with just
one more year to go. And no matter what
grade you're in, some of you are probably
wishing it were still summer, and you
could've stayed in bed just a little longer this
morning.

I know that feeling. When I was
young, my family lived in Indonesia for a few
years, and my mother didn't have the money
to send me where all the American kids went
to school. So she decided to teach me extra
lessons herself, Monday through Friday – at
4:30 in the morning.

129

Now I wasn't too happy about getting up that early. A lot of times, I'd fall asleep right there at the kitchen table. But whenever I'd complain, my mother would just give me one of those looks and say, "This is no picnic for me either, buster."

So I know some of you are still adjusting to being back at school. But I'm here today because I have something important to discuss with you. I'm here because I want to talk with you about your education and what's expected of all of you in this new school year.

Now I've given a lot of speeches about education. And I've talked a lot about responsibility.

I've talked about your teachers' responsibility for inspiring you, and pushing you to learn.

I've talked about your parents' responsibility for making sure you stay on track, and get your homework done, and don't spend every waking hour in front of the TV or with that Xbox.

I've talked a lot about your government's responsibility for setting high standards, supporting teachers and principals, and turning around schools that aren't working where students aren't getting the opportunities they deserve.

But at the end of the day, we can have the most dedicated teachers, the most supportive parents, and the best schools in the world – and none of it will matter unless all of you fulfill your responsibilities. Unless you show up to those schools; pay attention to those teachers; listen to your parents, grandparents and other adults; and put in the hard work it takes to succeed.

And that's what I want to focus on today: the responsibility each of you has for your education. I want to start with the responsibility you have to yourself.

Every single one of you has something you're good at. Every single one of you has something to offer. And you have a responsibility to yourself to discover what that is. That's the opportunity an education can provide.

Maybe you could be a good writer – maybe even good enough to write a book or articles in a newspaper – but you might not know it until you write a paper for your English class. Maybe you could be an innovator or an inventor – maybe even good enough to come up with the next iPhone or a new medicine or vaccine – but you might not know it until you do a project for your science class. Maybe you could be a mayor or a Senator or a Supreme Court Justice, but you might not know that until you join student government or the debate team.

And no matter what you want to do with your life – I guarantee that you'll need an education to do it. You want to be a doctor, or a teacher, or a police officer? You want to be a nurse or an architect, a lawyer or a member of our military? You're going to need a good education for every single one of those careers. You can't drop out of school and just drop into a good job. You've got to work for it and train for it and learn for it.

And this isn't just important for your own life and your own future. What you make of your education will decide nothing less than the future of this country. What you're learning in school today will determine whether we as a nation can meet our greatest challenges in the future.

You'll need the knowledge and problem-solving skills you learn in science and math to cure diseases like cancer and AIDS, and to develop new energy technologies and protect our environment. You'll need the insights and critical thinking skills you gain in history and social studies to fight poverty and homelessness, crime and discrimination, and make our nation more fair and more free. You'll need the creativity and ingenuity you develop in all your classes to build new companies that will create new jobs and boost our economy.

We need every single one of you to develop your talents, skills and intellect so you can help solve our most difficult problems. If you don't do that – if you quit on school – you're not just quitting on yourself, you're quitting on your country.

Now I know it's not always easy to do well in school. I know a lot of you have challenges in your lives right now that can make it hard to focus on your schoolwork.

I get it. I know what that's like. My father left my family when I was two years old, and I was raised by a single mother who struggled at times to pay the bills and wasn't always able to give us things the other kids had. There were times when I missed having a father in my life. There were times when I was lonely and felt like I didn't fit in.

So I wasn't always as focused as I should have been. I did some things I'm not proud of, and got in more trouble than I should have. And my life could have easily taken a turn for the worse.

But I was fortunate. I got a lot of second chances and had the opportunity to go to college, and law school, and follow my dreams. My wife, our First Lady Michelle Obama, has a similar story. Neither of her parents had gone to college, and they didn't have much. But they worked hard, and she worked hard, so that she could go to the best schools in this country.

Some of you might not have those advantages. Maybe you don't have adults in your life who give you the support that you need. Maybe someone in your family has lost their job, and there's not enough money to go around. Maybe you live in a neighborhood where you don't feel safe, or have friends who are pressuring you to do things you know aren't right.

But at the end of the day, the circumstances of your life – what you look like, where you come from, how much money you have, what you've got going on at home – that's no excuse for neglecting your homework or having a bad attitude. That's no excuse for talking back to your teacher, or cutting class, or dropping out of school. That's no excuse for not trying.

Where you are right now doesn't have to determine where you'll end up. No one's written your destiny for you. Here in America, you write your own destiny. You make your own future.

That's what young people like you are doing every day, all across America.

Young people like Jazmin Perez, from Roma, Texas. Jazmin didn't speak English when she first started school. Hardly anyone in her hometown went to college, and neither of her parents had gone either. But she worked hard, earned good grades, got a scholarship to Brown University, and is now in graduate school, studying public health, on her way to being Dr. Jazmin Perez.

I'm thinking about Andoni Schultz, from Los Altos, California, who's fought brain cancer since he was three. He's endured all sorts of treatments and surgeries, one of which affected his memory, so it took him much longer – hundreds of extra hours – to do his schoolwork. But he never fell behind, and he's headed to college this fall.

And then there's Shantell Steve, from my hometown of Chicago, Illinois. Even when bouncing from foster home to foster home in the toughest neighborhoods, she managed to get a job at a local health center; start a program to keep young people out of gangs; and she's on track to graduate high school with honors and go on to college.

Jazmin, Andoni and Shantell aren't any different from any of you. They faced challenges in their lives just like you do. But they refused to give up. They chose to take responsibility for their education and set goals for themselves. And I expect all of you to do the same.

That's why today, I'm calling on each of you to set your own goals for your education – and to do everything you can to meet them. Your goal can be something as simple as doing all your homework, paying attention in class, or spending time each day reading a book. Maybe you'll decide to get involved in an extracurricular activity, or volunteer in your community. Maybe you'll decide to stand up for kids who are being teased or bullied because of who they are or how they look, because you believe, like I do, that all kids deserve a safe environment to study and learn. Maybe you'll decide to take better care of yourself so you can be more ready to learn. And along those lines, I hope you'll all wash your hands a lot, and stay home from school when you don't feel well, so we can keep people from getting the flu this fall and winter.

Whatever you resolve to do, I want you to commit to it. I want you to really work at it.

I know that sometimes, you get the sense from TV that you can be rich and successful without any hard work -- that your ticket to success is through rapping or basketball or being a reality TV star, when chances are, you're not going to be any of those things.

But the truth is, being successful is hard. You won't love every subject you study. You won't click with every teacher. Not every homework assignment will seem completely relevant to your life right this minute. And you won't necessarily succeed at everything the first time you try.

That's OK. Some of the most successful people in the world are the ones who've had the most failures. JK Rowling's first Harry Potter book was rejected twelve times before it was finally published. Michael Jordan was cut from his high school basketball team, and he lost hundreds of games and missed thousands of shots during his career. But he once said, "I have failed over and over and over again in my life. And that is why I succeed."

These people succeeded because they understand that you can't let your failures define you – you have to let them teach you. You have to let them show you what to do differently next time. If you get in trouble, that doesn't mean you're a troublemaker, it means you need to try harder to behave. If you get a bad grade, that doesn't mean you're stupid, it just means you need to spend more time studying.

No one's born being good at things, you become good at things through hard work. You're not a varsity athlete the first time you play a new sport. You don't hit every note the first time you sing a song. You've got to practice. It's the same with your schoolwork. You might have to do a math problem a few times before you get it right, or read something a few times before you understand it, or do a few drafts of a paper before it's good enough to hand in.

Don't be afraid to ask questions. Don't be afraid to ask for help when you need it. I do that every day. Asking for help isn't a sign of weakness, it's a sign of strength. It shows you have the courage to admit when you don't know something, and to learn something new. So find an adult you trust – a parent, grandparent or teacher; a coach or counselor – and ask them to help you stay on track to meet your goals.

And even when you're struggling, even when you're discouraged, and you feel

like other people have given up on you –
don't ever give up on yourself. Because when
you give up on yourself, you give up on your
country.

The story of America isn't about
people who quit when things got tough. It's
about people who kept going, who tried
harder, who loved their country too much to
do anything less than their best.

It's the story of students who sat
where you sit 250 years ago, and went on to
wage a revolution and found this
nation. Students who sat where you sit 75
years ago who overcame a Depression and
won a world war; who fought for civil rights
and put a man on the moon. Students who sat
where you sit 20 years ago who founded
Google, Twitter and Facebook and changed
the way we communicate with each other.

So today, I want to ask you, what's
your contribution going to be? What problems
are you going to solve? What discoveries will
you make? What will a president who comes
here in twenty or fifty or one hundred years
say about what all of you did for this
country?

Your families, your teachers, and I are
doing everything we can to make sure you
have the education you need to answer these
questions. I'm working hard to fix up your
classrooms and get you the books, equipment
and computers you need to learn. But you've
got to do your part too. So I expect you to get

serious this year. I expect you to put your best effort into everything you do. I expect great things from each of you. So don't let us down – don't let your family or your country or yourself down. Make us all proud. I know you can do it.

Thank you, God bless you, and God bless America.

One school district in Texas did not show the President's address in its schools and students had to go to a church to see the speech. It was later revealed that the same district was planning to bus a group of fifth-grade students to an event at the Dallas Cowboy's stadium where one of the scheduled speakers was former President George W. Bush. The school district in question later cancelled the trip after it drew considerable negative media attention.

President Obama delivered a speech to students on September 8, 2009, about the importance of exercising personal responsibility, perseverance and doing well in school. The reality made all of the pre-speech hysteria and ranting seem ridiculous. There were a certain group of people in a preemptive objection mode when it came to anything Barack Obama planned to undertake. That was where we were as a country eight months into the term of the first African American President of the United States and it was a sad place to occupy.

Even after the positive, well received and uplifting message that Barack Obama gave to students, some still refused to back down. Some opponents harped on a prior lesson plan that had been changed. One critic said the message was good, but he made the speech about himself while others insisted that he had changed the original text. It was clear that most of the objections were about the messenger regardless of the message.

Chapter 18

♦

Things were becoming uncomfortable seven
months into the presidency of Barack Obama.
Political commentators were searching for
words and reasons for the vocal opposition to
virtually everything the President, who was
elected by a wide margin, proposed. Given
that the makeup of the news media was
largely composed of non-African Americans,
it became a virtual verbal squirm festival.
After a prolonged barrage of negativity aimed
at President Obama, some in the media asked
the rhetorical question, "Is this about his
race?"

Some finally acknowledged the
elephant that was sitting in the middle of the

room. It was clearly a painful exercise for many commentating on current events to voice concerns that race was the underlying factor in how some citizens, other media personalities and even politicians were reacting to President Obama. No one from the conservative political leadership camp was calling for moderation. The silence was deafening and disturbing.

The voices that seemed to be speaking for the Republican Party were comprised of a strange collection of talk-show hosts, formerly obscure politicians and borderline extremists. At the top of the list was former Governor of Alaska, Sarah Palin, who helped spread the misconception that Obama's health-care plan included death panels.

Another voice of division came from Minnesota Congresswoman Michelle Bachman who said President Obama wanted to send young people to reeducation camps. Bachman also told a group of supporters that they needed to all slit their wrists and become blood brothers to stop health-care reform.

Michelle Malkin, a popular conservative blogger, who appeared on the Today Show on NBC on July 29, 2009. Malkin called President Obama a racial opportunist and referred to Michelle Obama as the crony in chief.

Then we get to the heavyweights when it comes to rhetoric against President Obama. Rush Limbaugh reportedly commands an audience in excess of twenty million radio listeners and he emerged as some sort of de facto Republican Party leader. Michael Steele, the head of the Republican National Committee, was asked on a national cable talk show about Limbaugh's status in the Republican Party. Steele said Limbaugh was an entertainer. Steele, while feeling the pressure of Limbaugh's ability to address the issue with his vast audience, called Rush and apologized. Limbaugh held no elected office and seemingly could say virtually anything he wanted without any fear of reprisal. Limbaugh, as mentioned earlier, aired the Barack The Magic Negro Song on his show and openly said that he wanted Obama to fail. If you recall it was during the Democratic Party Primary contest when Limbaugh called for his listeners, who were often called "dittoheads", to vote for Hillary Clinton. Limbaugh wanted to extend the primaries so Hillary could continue to bring Obama down and weaken him as a general election candidate. Obviously that strategy did not work.

Glenn Beck practiced a special mix of paranoia laced theatrics that appealed to a large audience of conservatives. Earlier in this book I stated that Beck called Barack Obama a "racist" who had a "deep-seated hatred for white people or the white culture." Beck seemed to dwell on conspiracy theories about how liberals were leading the country to ruin.

The fact that Barack Obama was President created a boom for the conservative news/entertainment business. Nothing increased demand like a common foe. Barack Obama was the ultimate common foe on multiple fronts. A testament to the lucrative nature of commercial conservatism was the example of amazon.com's top-two bestselling nonfiction books on September 7, 2009, were by Glenn Beck and Michelle Malkin. While the conservative noise machine railed against Obama, they secretly rejoiced at his election because of the business opportunities it had afforded them.

Whenever there is a large group of frustrated individuals with a similar grievance, there is an opportunity for exploitation. The decisive win by Obama was not good enough for many who voted against him. A vocal group of disaffected voters were rejecting the election results. Those people were ripe for exploitation by conservative profiteers who would willingly tell them what they wanted to hear, for a price.

Chapter 19

♦

What the United States now knows as Social Security was enacted in 1935 by President Franklin Roosevelt and became his lasting legacy. Senior citizens across the country depend on monthly Social Security payments as an essential economic safety net.

In 1965 President Lyndon Johnson signed amendments to the Social Security act that brought Medicare into existence. Medicare is a mainstay in the lives of senior citizens and how millions receive their health care. Medicare became the lasting legacy of President Johnson.

President Barack Obama was attempting to carve his name into the wall of presidential legacy by delivering on providing health care for all Americans. Health care for all Americans had been a goal that had eluded Presidents for decades. The following are excerpts of President Barack Obama's speech to a joint session of Congress September 9, 2009:

THE WHITE HOUSE
Office of the Press Secretary

For Immediate Release ,
September 9, 2009
EXCERPTS OF THE PRESIDENT'S ADDRESS TO A JOINT SESSION OF CONGRESS TONIGHT:

I am not the first President to take up this cause, but I am determined to be the last. It has now been nearly a century since Theodore Roosevelt first called for health care reform. And ever since, nearly every President and Congress, whether Democrat or Republican, has attempted to meet this challenge in some way. A bill for comprehensive health reform was first introduced by John Dingell Sr. in 1943. Sixty-five years later, his son continues to introduce that same bill at the beginning of each session.

Our collective failure to meet this challenge – year after year, decade after decade – has led us to a breaking point.

146

Everyone understands the extraordinary hardships that are placed on the uninsured, who live every day just one accident or illness away from bankruptcy. These are not primarily people on welfare. These are middle-class Americans. Some can't get insurance on the job. Others are self-employed, and can't afford it, since buying insurance on your own costs you three times as much as the coverage you get from your employer. Many other Americans who are willing and able to pay are still denied insurance due to previous illnesses or conditions that insurance companies decide are too risky or expensive to cover.

***

During that time, we have seen Washington at its best and its worst.

We have seen many in this chamber work tirelessly for the better part of this year to offer thoughtful ideas about how to achieve reform. Of the five committees asked to develop bills, four have completed their work, and the Senate Finance Committee announced today that it will move forward next week. That has never happened before. Our overall efforts have been supported by an unprecedented coalition of doctors and nurses; hospitals, seniors' groups and even drug companies – many of whom opposed reform in the past. And there is agreement in this chamber on about eighty percent of what needs to be done, putting us closer to the goal of reform than we have ever been.

But what we have also seen in these last months is the same partisan spectacle that only hardens the disdain many Americans have toward their own government. Instead of honest debate, we have seen scare tactics. Some have dug into unyielding ideological camps that offer no hope of compromise. Too many have used this as an opportunity to score short-term political points, even if it robs the country of our opportunity to solve a long-term challenge. And out of this blizzard of charges and counter-charges, confusion has reigned.

Well the time for bickering is over. The time for games has passed. Now is the season for action. Now is when we must bring the best ideas of both parties together, and show the American people that we can still do what we were sent here to do. Now is the time to deliver on health care.

The plan I'm announcing tonight would meet three basic goals:

It will provide more security and stability to those who have health insurance. It will provide insurance to those who don't. And it will slow the growth of health care costs for our families, our businesses, and our government. It's a plan that asks everyone to take responsibility for meeting this challenge – not just government and insurance companies, but employers and individuals.

And it's a plan that incorporates ideas from Senators and Congressmen; from Democrats and Republicans – and yes, from some of my opponents in both the primary and general election.

***

Here are the details that every American needs to know about this plan:

First, if you are among the hundreds of millions of Americans who already have health insurance through your job, Medicare, Medicaid, or the VA, nothing in this plan will require you or your employer to change the coverage or the doctor you have. Let me repeat this: nothing in our plan requires you to change what you have.

What this plan will do is to make the insurance you have work better for you. Under this plan, it will be against the law for insurance companies to deny you coverage because of a pre-existing condition. As soon as I sign this bill, it will be against the law for insurance companies to drop your coverage when you get sick or water it down when you need it most. They will no longer be able to place some arbitrary cap on the amount of coverage you can receive in a given year or a lifetime. We will place a limit on how much you can be charged for out-of-pocket expenses, because in the United States of America, no one should go broke because they get sick. And insurance companies will be required to cover, with no extra charge, routine checkups and preventive care, like mammograms and colonoscopies – because there's no reason we shouldn't be catching diseases like breast cancer and colon cancer before they get worse. That makes sense, it saves money, and it saves lives.

That's what Americans who have health insurance can expect from this plan – more security and stability.

Now, if you're one of the tens of millions of Americans who don't currently have health insurance, the second part of this plan will finally offer you quality, affordable choices. If you lose your job or change your job, you will be able to get coverage. If you strike out on your own and start a small business, you will be able to get coverage. We will do this by creating a new insurance exchange – a marketplace where individuals and small businesses will be able to shop for health insurance at competitive prices. Insurance companies will have an incentive to participate in this exchange because it lets them compete for millions of new customers. As one big group, these customers will have greater leverage to bargain with the insurance companies for better prices and quality coverage. This is how large companies and government employees get affordable insurance. It's how everyone in this Congress gets affordable insurance. And it's time to give every American the same opportunity that we've given ourselves.

***

This is the plan I'm proposing. It's a plan that incorporates ideas from many of the people in this room tonight – Democrats and Republicans. And I will continue to seek common ground in the weeks ahead. If you come to me with a serious set of proposals, I will be there to listen. My door is always open.

But know this: I will not waste time with those who have made the calculation that it's better politics to kill this plan than improve it. I will not stand by while the special interests use the same old tactics to keep things exactly the way they are. If you misrepresent what's in the plan, we will call you out. And I will not accept the status quo as a solution. Not this time. Not now.

Everyone in this room knows what will happen if we do nothing. Our deficit will grow. More families will go bankrupt. More businesses will close. More Americans will lose their coverage when they are sick and need it most. And more will die as a result. We know these things to be true.

That is why we cannot fail. Because there are too many Americans counting on us to succeed – the ones who suffer silently, and the ones who shared their stories with us at town hall meetings, in emails, and in letters.

On September 9, 2009, President Barack Obama answered many of his critics face to face and promised to call them out in the future. Obama called the assertion that his health-care plan included death panels a lie.

Even in the midst of that nationally televised speech, discord and disrespect was displayed for all to hear. President Obama stated that the assertion that his health-care plan would cover illegal immigrants was not true. South Carolina Republican Congressman Joe Wilson yelled, "You lie!" That was the ultimate in disrespect, but it was a rare explosion of personal contempt on a national stage.

The media, Democrats and Republicans ripped Wilson for his conduct. Wilson quickly apologized, but seemed to do so only because he was asked by the Republican leadership. Wilson seemed to have no true remorse for his incredible show of disrespect to President Obama. Wilson was also caught on camera yelling his unbelievable insult at the commander-in-chief. It was reported that Wilson's opponent for the next election received one million dollars in donations over the days following the incident. Wilson, who vowed that he would not be muzzled, received over 700 thousand dollars in contributions.

Barack Obama pushed back hard against the storm of opposition. Even as his voice was still echoing in the hall, his critics were revving up their attack machine for the next round.

Chapter 20

♦

Barack Obama became the forty-fourth President of the United States by walking a tightrope over a pit filled with historical quicksand. Obama did not win by a fluke, but by running the most efficient campaign in the history of United States presidential politics.

The coalition that elected Barack Obama was the most diverse that this country had seen in a presidential contest. A collection of young, old, white, black, Hispanic, wealthy and poor elected the first black American President into office. Almost seventy million voters swept Barack Obama into office, but almost sixty million people voted for John McCain. Some of the votes for

McCain were anti-Obama votes. Unlike the 2000 election when the candidate with more popular votes lost the electoral vote battle and George W. Bush became President instead of Al Gore. Obama won by a decisive margin with over nine and one-half million more popular votes and 192 more electoral votes. With that kind of mandate from the American people, why was there such bitterness towards the President emanating from some quarters?

As mentioned earlier the answer is found deep within the group that did not vote for Obama. This was not a case of I like my candidate but if the other guy wins, so be it. The presidential election of 2008 was a stark contrast affair. Many who voted against Obama could under no circumstances see themselves voting for him. What developed was a schism in the electorate as wide as the Grand Canyon. Many who voted for McCain saw Obama voters as misguided and unpatriotic instead of just having a difference of opinion. Some probably viewed white Obama supporters as traitors to their race as they voted for a black man for President. How could they hand the country over to blacks, liberals and immigrants? Instead of having a soft opposition that he could win over, the new President faced a hard core of opposition who had closed ears, minds and hearts to his message because of who the messenger was.

Just who is Barack Obama and how would he handle such ingrained opposition?

Barack Obama had demonstrated that he was a deceptively tough and resilient politician with a very savvy team around him. I would consider President Obama to be a political counter puncher. Instead of engaging in transactional back and forth battles with individual opponents, he allows his antagonists to fully extend and reveal themselves before striking back. If you consider that he is a highly skilled lawyer, then his mode of operation seems natural. Any litigator would love to get all of the evidence in before attacking each element separately and knocking it down.

Consider how the campaign unfolded. With the Reverend Wright flap, Obama allowed the media and other contenders to hammer away and bring the issue to a head. When the controversy reached a crescendo, Obama focused the attention of the media world and answered with his seminal speech on race in Philadelphia. Later he handled a Reverend Wright flare up by distancing himself from his former pastor.

If you examine each pivotal moment of danger for the former senator from Illinois, he executed a similar calm plan, gathered all available information and reacted.

When the economy collapsed near the end of 2008, Obama remained calm before and after the election. As the economy lost hundreds of thousands of jobs per month, there was ample opportunity for panic within the population, but the calm demeanor of the President helped to steady the nation. Let us not forget the H1N1 swine-flu pandemic. Schools were closed and there was no vaccine in sight. Panic did not ensue and the calm demeanor of the commander-in-chief helped to steady citizens.

Considering the barrage of problems that had battered the United States since Obama's inauguration, there were ample opportunities for hysteria. It is amazing how a nation can take on the demeanor of its leaders. The United States appears to have adopted the calmness of its President. The country had decided that it was reasonable to expect it to take some time for the country to extricate itself from a set of issues that took years to develop.

The howling winds of ugly opposition had begun to blow. Critics opposed to anything the President proposed had whipped their troops into an almost mindless frenzy. As a debate on reforming the nation's national health-care system raged with shouting mobs roaming from one town-hall meeting to another. The hatred even claimed collateral victims. Congressman David Scott of Georgia found the sign outside of his district office in Smyrna, Georgia vandalized with a four-foot spray-painted swastika. This occurred after a contentious town-hall meeting on health-care reform.

August 2009

While it was very clear that winds of change had roared across the political landscape. It was also clear that attempts to repair a broken economy and health-care system allowed President Obama's critics to sit back and say no to every proposal. The necessity to address pressing issues also provided a lightning rod and permission slip for individuals to focus their hate. President Obama's signature is gracing some of the largest spending measures in American history. We knew whoever wielded the presidential pen determined where our national treasure flowed. Why did the idea of our wealth going to benefit people over corporations create so much outrage? Of course the answer was that a community organizer made his way into the White House and he attempted to help ordinary Americans instead of enriching the wealthy. Those with their hands on the reigns of power would not loosen their grip without a fight. Some who opposed the President for deep-seated personal reasons allowed their prejudices to enable themselves to be used to fight against their personal better interests.

The die was cast. Jim Crow was dead and its shadow was suffering a screaming demise as a new day dawned. President Barack Obama was a part of history and any actions in the future would not change that reality.

Barack Obama had a different set of expectations placed on him by history and the state of the nation. When he made his victory speech in Grant Park in Chicago on election night in 2008, he reached out to those who supported his opponent and said, "I will be your President too." Some accepted that assurance and quietly supported the new President while others did not. The country was facing economic problems that placed even more weight on the shoulders of the President-elect and generated greater expectations from his supporters.

President Obama gets that special judgment from his critics reserved for a select few. There will be endless blame for everything that goes wrong and scant credit for anything that works. That downside-only evaluation is reserved for those deemed to be undeserving of the position they hold. When the economy displayed promise of some life, there was silence. Any wild falsehood that discredited the President was given unwarranted credibility with tepid acknowledgement of facts emerging to debunk the prior claims.

The issue those still resistant needed to examine was their motives. We are a great country that seems to have developed a strange phobia. How did the United States of America become a nation in fear of doing exactly what many claim they want to do, take our country back? The groups that we needed to take our country back from were corporate entities that had bled its citizens dry for years. How many outsourced jobs will it take? How many citizens denied health insurance coverage because of preexisting conditions will it take? How many low-wage jobs replacing high salaried positions will it take? How many hundreds of millions of dollars in compensation for corporate CEOs will it require before eyes that have no problem seeing black and white begin to see red? Stop in your tracks and try and determine why you are angry and shouting. Is it for your best interest or for the betterment of others to your detriment?

During the presidential campaign, Senator Ted Kennedy not only endorsed Obama, but he literally passed the baton of political legacy from the Kennedy clan and placed it into the hand of Barack Obama. Somehow Senator Kennedy knew that his time was short. Later in 2008 he was diagnosed with brain cancer. Senator Edward Kennedy died On August 25, 2009 and President Barack Obama delivered his eulogy on August 29, 2009. Kennedy's greatest political struggle over the years, health care for all Americans, was in the middle of a bitter debate at the time of his death, and the man carrying the ball was President Barack Obama.

A President does not have the option of only helping those who supported him, but is charged do what is best for everyone. What Barack Obama was going through as the first black President was something no one else could ever know. As he attempted to help those who rooted for his failure, we all knew one thing. Obama's path to the White House began in the bellies of slave ships and detoured through the Underground Railroad. Stepping stones that lead to 1600 Pennsylvania Avenue were paved with unmarked graves, civil war grave markers and fallen heroes of other great wars. The final ascent to the oval office was made by scaling to the mountain's peak with blood soaked ropes that once hung from lynching trees. Obama's father came directly from Kenya and his mother was from Kansas, but their son was tied into the legacy of all black Americans. Yes, Barack Obama had been judged Guilty of Being President While Black, did we expect anything different?

Godspeed, Mr. President.

About The Author

ESSENCE® bestselling author D.T. Pollard lives in the Dallas/Fort Worth, TX area. He is married and has one son.

He earned an academic scholarship to the School of Business and Industry at Florida A & M University. He stopped writing during his second year in college.

D T was at the top of his class in Marketing and graduated Summa Cum Laude and won the Most-Outstanding-Performance-in-Marketing award for his graduating class of 1981.

While working in sales for giants of the high-technology world for over 28 years, his desire to write returned after losing several siblings from various causes. D T Pollard is the author of Rooftop Diva - A Novel of Triumph After Katrina, Fools' Heaven – Love, Lust and Death beyond the Pulpit and TARP Town U S A – The Recession That Saved America.

OBAMA – GUILTY – of Being President While Black - takes a unique look at the racism faced by President Barack Obama and how vestiges of Jim Crow laws infested the thoughts of many people today.

www.DTPollard.com

Air Force One

Obama Limo

Senator Barack Obama (D-Ill.), rebounds the ball during a basketball game with U.S. military service members from Combined Joint Task Force-Horn of Africa during his visit at Camp Lemonier, Djibouti, on Aug. 31, 2006.

Democratic U.S. Presidential candidate
Barack Obama on stage with the late Senator
Ted Kennedy, at the XL Center in downtown
Hartford, Connecticut.

February 4, 2008

Image Source: Wikipedia.org
Photo Author: Ragesoss

Barack Obama speaking at a campaign rally
in Abington, PA

Image source:
http://en.wikipedia.org/wiki/File:ObamaAbin
gtonPA.JPG
Uploaded by: Bbsrock

Barack Obama delivering his victory speech
on Election Night ´08, in Grant Park, Chicago

Image Source:
http://en.wikipedia.org/wiki/File:
Obama08acceptance.jpg uploaded by Gabbec

President George W. Bush and
Barack Obama meet in Oval Office

Then President of the United States of
America, George W. Bush invited then
President-Elect Barack Obama and former
Presidents George H.W. Bush, Bill Clinton,
and Jimmy Carter for a meeting and lunch at
The White House. Jan. 7, 2009

Official presidential portrait of
Barack Obama

Taken by: Pete Souza, The Obama-Biden
Transition Project

Useful Information Sources

http://www.nps.gov/malu/index.htm

http://www.huffingtpost.com/

http://www.msnbc.com

http://cnn.com

http://www.about.com

http://www.wikipedia.org

http://fec.gov

http://www.whitehouse.gov/